W0036004

ADVANCE PRAISE

Parsa Venkateshwar Rao offers a lucid and wide-ranging analysis of the momentous changes that have transformed the Indian economy and society and the challenges that the political system has to cope with after economic reforms and the rise of majoritarianism. Written in an accessible and cogent style, this book will serve as a useful introduction for understanding some of the key political developments that have impacted democracy in the last 30 years.

Zoya Hasan, *Professor Emerita, Centre for Political Studies, Jawaharlal Nehru University, New Delhi*

Parsa Venkateshwar Rao describes India's turbulent history of the past decades but concentrating almost exclusively on economic reforms and the rise of Hindu fundamentalism, the first portrayed as necessary and the second as populist electoral adventurism. Concentrating on policy statements and debates, he ventures into the unenviable look of assessing contemporary history. Philosophers warn that the owl of Minerva's wisdom flies after the twilight. Parsa wants us to turn to present continuities. He does this with acuity. This book should be read by those who know and need to review what they know and those who want to know.

Rajeev Dhavan, *Supreme Court Advocate*

The past shapes the present in both direct and tangential ways and provides an understanding of our times. Combining the strengths of a scholar of politics and that of an observer journalist, Parsa Venkateshwar Rao Jr seeks to capture a crucial period in India's political history, bookended by two prime ministers, Rajiv Gandhi and Narendra Modi. The book provides important insights into the often overlapping processes of economic reforms and political Hinduism that came to dominate this three-decade period in ways that irrevocably changed India.

Pamela Philipose, *Public Editor,* The Wire

Tough-minded journalism demands a sense of openness, a power of judgement and a ruthless sense of professionalism. It requires both a relentless sense of facts and an unflagging sense of judgement. Parsa Rao combines these qualities in a book that traverses across two eras, the age of Rajiv Gandhi and the Modi era. In comparing the two, he creates a choreography of different styles of politics, bringing out the differences and limits of each era.

Rao is demanding as a writer, insisting that the reader think through the book with him. Quietly nuanced, the book is an invitation to rethink the fate of policy, politics and democracy. A narrative which spans 35 years of politics captures every moment of change from Rajiv's assassination, Babri, the Gujarat riots to Modi's ascent, Rao creates a tough titrated vision of political dynamics. A distilled insight into a noisy era full of drama of possibilities and limits.

Shiv Visvanathan, *Professor, O.P. Jindal*
Global University, Haryana

RAJIV
GANDHI

to

NARENDRA
MODI

RAJIV GANDHI

to

NARENDRA MODI

Broken Polity, Flickering Reforms

Parsa Venkateshwar Rao Jr

Los Angeles | London | New Delhi
Singapore | Washington DC | Melbourne

First published in 2019 by

SAGE Publications India Pvt Ltd
B1/I-1 Mohan Cooperative Industrial Area
Mathura Road, New Delhi 110 044, India
www.sagepub.in

SAGE Publications Inc
2455 Teller Road
Thousand Oaks, California 91320, USA

SAGE Publications Ltd
1 Oliver's Yard, 55 City Road
London EC1Y 1SP, United Kingdom

SAGE Publications Asia-Pacific Pte Ltd
18 Cross Street #10-10/11/12
China Square Central
Singapore 048423

Published by Vivek Mehra for SAGE Publications India Pvt Ltd, typeset in 9.5/13.5 pts ITC Stone Serif by Fidus Design Pvt. Ltd, Chandigarh.

Library of Congress Cataloging-in-Publication Data Available

ISBN: 978-93-532-8298-1 (PB)

SAGE Team: Manisha Mathews, Guneet Kaur Gulati, Syeda Aina Rahat Ali, Rajinder Kaur

To my elder sister,
Parsa Alimelu Manga Tayar,
for her silent sacrifices

Thank you for choosing a SAGE product!
If you have any comment, observation or feedback,
I would like to personally hear from you.

Please write to me at **contactceo@sagepub.in**

Vivek Mehra, Managing Director and CEO, SAGE India.

Bulk Sales

SAGE India offers special discounts
for purchase of books in bulk.
We also make available special imprints
and excerpts from our books on demand.

For orders and enquiries, write to us at

Marketing Department
SAGE Publications India Pvt Ltd
B1/I-1, Mohan Cooperative Industrial Area
Mathura Road, Post Bag 7
New Delhi 110044, India

E-mail us at **marketing@sagepub.in**

Subscribe to our mailing list

Write to **marketing@sagepub.in**

This book is also available as an e-book.

CONTENTS

LIST OF ABBREVIATIONS

AAGSP	All Assam Gana Sangram Parishad
AASU	All Assam Students Union
AGP	Asom Gana Parishad
AIADMK	All India Anna Dravida Munnetra Kazhagam
AIBMAC	All India Babri Masjid Action Committee
AICC	All India Congress Committee
BIFR	Board for Industrial and Financial Reconstruction
BJP	Bharatiya Janata Party
BJS	Bharatiya Jana Sangh
BPO	business process outsourcing
CAG	Comptroller and Auditor General
CBI	Central Bureau of Investigation
CII	Confederation of Indian Industry
CPB	Central Parliamentary Board
CPI	Communist Party of India
CPI(M)	Communist Party of India (Marxist)
CPP	Congress Parliamentary Party
CPSU	Communist Party of the Soviet Union
CTBT	Comprehensive Nuclear-Test-Ban Treaty
CVC	Chief Vigilance Commissioner
CWC	Congress Working Committee
DMK	Dravida Munnetra Kazhagam
DoT	Department of Telecommunications
FBG	financial bank guarantee
GATT	General Agreement on Tariffs and Trade
GST	Goods and Services Tax
IAEA	International Atomic Energy Agency
ICHR	Indian Council of Historical Research
IFS	Indian Foreign Service
IMF	International Monetary Fund
IPKF	Indian Peace Keeping Force

IT	information technology
IUML	Indian Union Muslim League
JP	Jayaprakash Narayan
JPC	Joint Parliamentary Committee
LoIs	letters of intent
LTTE	Liberation Tigers of Tamil Eelam
MGNREGA	Mahatma Gandhi National Rural Employment Guarantee Act
MIM	Majlis-e-Ittehadul Muslimeen
MNF	Mizo National Front
MP	member of parliament
NAC	National Advisory Council
NCMP	National Common Minimum Programme
NDA	National Democratic Alliance
NIC	National Integration Council
NPAs	non-performing assets
NPT	Non-Proliferation Treaty
NSSP	Next Steps in Strategic Partnerships
OBCs	Other Backward Classes
OIC	Organisation of Islamic Countries
PAC	Public Accounts Committee
PBG	performance bank guarantee
PIB	Press Information Bureau
PIL	public interest litigation
R&AW	Research and Analysis Wing
RSP	Revolutionary Socialist Party
RSS	Rashtriya Swayamsevak Sangh
SAARC	South Asian Association for Regional Cooperation
SAD	Shiromani Akali Dal
SGPC	Shiromani Gurdwara Prabandhak Committee
SIT	Special Investigation Team
SP	Samajwadi Party
SVD	Samyukta Vidhayak Dal
TDP	Telugu Desam Party
TRAI	Telecom Regulatory Authority of India
UF	United Front
UPA	United Progressive Alliance

USSR	Union of Soviet Socialist Republics
VHP	Vishva Hindu Parishad
WB	World Bank
WMD	weapons of mass destruction
WTO	World Trade Organization

FOREWORD

Change and Permanence in Indian Politics

The French have an expression which translates as 'The more things change, the more they stay the same.' Over the coming months, as rival coalitions battle for the majority in Lok Sabha, the focus will be on a single person, Narendra Modi. His supporters will say that he has been a breath of fresh air and he removed the Nehruvian cobwebs, advanced India's image in the world, battled corruption and laid the foundations for a Hindu *rashtra* (nation). His detractors would say that he has shattered the old tolerant democratic consensus, failed to deliver on tall promises and mired the economy in unemployment and stagnation. They will add that corruption is as bad as it ever was, if not worse.

This much is pretty routine in any election battle. But the issue remains that how unique a political leader Narendra Modi is. Parsa Venkateshwar has had the brilliant idea of doing a comparative study of Rajiv Gandhi and Narendra Modi. At first, it sounds strange. What can there be common between a scion of the Nehru–Gandhi dynasty and a Rashtriya Swayamsevak Sangh (RSS) *pracharak* (preacher), except that they were born three years either side of the iconic year 1947?

Rajiv Gandhi was the last member of the dynasty to be prime minister and also someone who won the largest number of seats and the highest vote share ever in the first election he fought. In the next election he fought, his party was the largest single party but failed to win majority. That result inaugurated 25 years of history where there were coalitions but no single-party majority. Narendra Modi broke that mould and won a single-party majority in 2014. The question in everyone's mind is: Will he win a majority again or go the Rajiv Gandhi way? Of course, Rajiv refused to form a coalition as that was a novel idea; Modi is already in a coalition which may win a majority in any case.

But there is more. Rajiv inaugurated the idea of neoliberal reform for the economy, though his family credentials were such that he did not have to make it look like a break with the past. His reforms did not yield immediate fruits (though the economy hit a double-digit growth rate in one year) and two years later, India had to pawn its gold reserves as it had run a massive deficit.

Modi comes at the stage when reform has become routine and the economy has become the fastest growing in the world and yet the cacophony of complaints about jobs and farmers' distress is persistent. Will the economy nosedive within the next two or three years?

The last parallel is about corruption. Rajiv Gandhi got caught in the Bofors scandal and his Finance Minister V.P. Singh turned against him and was a major factor in the loss of seats Rajiv suffered in 1989. Within the last six months, Rahul Gandhi has raised the question of likely corruption in the Rafale contract. Will Rahul succeed in inflicting damage on Narendra Modi?

But even so, India has changed profoundly in the 35 years which separate the 1984 election and the forthcoming 2019 election. Parsa takes us through this period of profound changes in the cultural politics of India as well as the changing political economy. He has delved extensively into the archives, and you get to read the words of the principal actors as they were spoken in Parliament and public over the years.

There are fascinating parliamentary debates about the Babri Masjid dispute as there are about the halting arrival of BJP into power after a failed attempt in 1996 and the hurried no-confidence motion of 1998. Economic issues come up constantly and remain the same. Only the personality of the finance minister changes. Yashwant Sinha and P. Chidambaram got to be finance minister twice for different coalitions. There are corruption scandals in each and every government and endless controversies. The system tries but does not quite succeed in eliminating corruption.

Let this book be your companion and guide as you try to make sense of the forthcoming tumultuous events in Indian politics.

Lord Meghnad Desai

PREFACE

The period that is covered in this book spans over 33 years, from the mid-1980s to near the end of the second decade of the 21st century. Someone born when Rajiv Gandhi took over as prime minister at the end of 1984 turned nearly 30 when Narendra Modi became prime minister in May 2014. I feel that two main issues that dominated this period were economic reforms and political Hinduism. Economic liberalization had ended socialism as we knew it, but it did not usher in political liberalism. Liberalization, surprisingly or unsurprisingly, brought in conservatism in politics and society.

There was the question: Was it P.V. Narasimha Rao who brought forth economic reforms in 1991 in the manner Zeus brought forth Athena from his head, or were the seeds of reforms sown much earlier? Many orthodox interpreters—political scientists and economists and journalists—hold the view that Rao is the Zeus-like progenitor of reforms, and this includes both who are opposed to and supportive of the shift to market economy. Again, those who applaud economic reforms are unable to explain the rise of political Hinduism in the form of rise of right-wing Bharatiya Janata Party (BJP) and its gradual electoral success, along with the festering issue of the Babri Masjid–Ram Janmabhoomi dispute in Ayodhya, located in the eastern corner of the backward state of Uttar Pradesh. So they pretend that politics is no more important in a post-ideological world as the 1991 reforms coincided with the fall of the 73-year-old communist Soviet Union and its satellite socialist states in Eastern Europe. But the record of the last 33 years shows that it is politics rooted in right-wing ideology of religious identity that caused much havoc in the country. For the leftist critics, the rise of right-wing politics alongside economic liberalization is interconnected.

It was the suggestion of Ms Manisha Mathews, Executive Editor at SAGE, that the book should cover the period from Rajiv Gandhi to Narendra Modi. The idea had an inherent attraction because it marks a period of history when many people and leaders were from a generation that did not experience the British rule and the freedom struggle. It was an independent India which was struggling to make sense of itself. Although Rajiv Gandhi and Narendra Modi continued to invoke Mahatma Gandhi, in practical terms the reality and the challenges of the day were quite different and the solutions that were being sought were perforce new. There was nothing catastrophic about this gentle break with this past, which was more a transition than a break. As time passed, it was but natural that the past—heroic and glorious—had to recede into a distant, if not fading memory, and the new generation could not any more hold on to the hem of history. Rajiv Gandhi was the first leader who spoke the language of a post-Independent India. He did not have sound answers to the issues of the time. India had to live in the present and look to the future, and it had to find its own solutions to its problems. It could not keep looking over its shoulder to the past. The importance of Rajiv Gandhi is that he stood at the vantage point of the present and future. He talked of India in a new, if naïve, language. He was not burdened with historical baggage. He spoke about economic reforms because he did not carry any ideological imprint of socialist politics in his thinking.

By the time Modi had come on the national scene as prime minister in 2014, economic reforms had been in place for a quarter century, and the idea of reforms was in play from 1985 onwards. In many ways, Modi had unwittingly become the inheritor of economic reforms. For young people of today, the term 'economic reforms' does not have the refreshing twang that it had for the youth of the 1980s and the 1990s. Talk of reforms has become jaded because today it is taken for granted that the engine of economic growth is not the state-run public sector corporations but the private sector and its big and small players. Economic reforms have run their course from a pre-reforms stage of the Rajiv Gandhi period through the post-reforms stage of Narendra Modi's prime ministerial term. India is a market, and not a socialist economy today, though Prime Minister Modi's governmental performance turns on welfare measures and pro-poor rhetoric but without the socialist tag.

There is the political story as well of the 30 years. And the major undercurrent is majoritarianism. Ironically, Rajiv Gandhi rode on the back of Hindu majoritarianism in the wake of the assassination of Indira Gandhi and the anti-Sikh riots that took place in Delhi and other urban centres of North India. Rajiv Gandhi was not a Hindu right-wing politician, but he showed no hesitation in using it for winning the 1984 Lok Sabha election. But it was not the ideological shield of either Rajiv Gandhi or Congress, while it was the natural armour of Modi and BJP. The ideological base of Modi's party, BJP, and its parental organization, RSS, is Hindu majoritarianism. Modi did not have to create it. He used it in winning three assembly elections in Gujarat in 2002, 2007 and 2012. He was the political icon of Hindutva. He did not harp on it in the 2014 Lok Sabha election because the popular mood was against the corruption-addled decade-old government of Prime Minister Manmohan Singh. But majoritarianism remained the undercurrent of the Modi/BJP victory of 2014, and despite protestations to the contrary from Modi and his colleagues in the government, the public mood from 2014 to 2018 remained majoritarian. There were no major Hindu–Muslim riots, but there were scores of stray incidents where Hindu mobs attacked ordinary and poor Muslims in towns and villages on charges of trading illegally in cows and for eating beef and killed some of the Muslims. These incidents revealed the ugly face of Hindutva, the neo-fascist ideology that the majority Hindus shall have the right of way.

This book is a political narrative which draws its information from 'official' sources—parliamentary debates, party documents, Budget speeches and economic surveys. I feel that this is one kind of narrative which needs to be written so that people can know the unnoticed details of the unfolding of history in the present. Here, the definition of history is taken as one which has occurred in the public domain, and that too on a recognized platform like the government. This is orthodox history in its narrow sense. It may not be the most tantalizing part on the face of it; but it remains an important part. The apparently unattractive official record has interesting and even explosive elements in its moth-eaten record, shreds and shards that reveal ideas and works underpinning the unrelenting tide of events that appear to be chaotic, without meaning and intent, as they float like flotsam and jetsam.

The number of people in any country, and especially in India, who have no interest in politics and who prefer to live their lives beyond the shadow of politics is huge. But the lives of the non-political and apolitical people are shaped by the politics of the day, and they are not aware of the impact. It can be compared to people living in quake-prone zones, where constant seismic buzz is lost on the consciousness of the inhabitants because they had internalized the noise. Political power games are the life-breath of politicians, but it is their words and deeds in decision-making bodies like parliament and in the government that affect people most. So politics and economics in the old-fashioned sense make and mar the lives of people living beyond the circles of power.

This book is an attempt to catch the wisps of politics and economics as articulated by politicians and policy-makers, and how they get reflected in larger outcomes such as electoral verdicts and economic growth rates and their components.

ACKNOWLEDGEMENTS

It has been possible to access the source material which forms the major part of this book because of the friendly and patient staff at the Gazettes and Debates Section of the Parliament Library. They include Indu Mannan, Dharmender, R.K. Tikku, Rakesh Bhatt and Pradeep Kumar Rai. It would have been impossible to get at the volumes without their wholehearted help. Thanks are also due to the staff at the Central Secretariat Library at Shastri Bhawan which houses the Lok Sabha and Rajya Sabha debates as well as the Budget speeches and economic surveys.

The Ministry of Finance, the Press Information Bureau and the Comptroller and Auditor General (CAG) of India websites have proved to be hugely fruitful. In the same way, the Allahabad High Court website was the place for the judgment in the Babri Masjid–Ram Janmabhoomi case delivered on 30 September 2010. The BJP and the Indian National Congress websites were useful as well.

I am much obliged to Lord Meghnad Desai for readily agreeing to write a short Foreword, and more than that for correcting the manuscript as he read through it. Most importantly, this book would not have happened without the initiative of Aarti David, Vice President, Publishing, SAGE. It has been a pleasure working with Production Editor Guneet Kaur and the Editorial team who sent innumerable queries about the text in their attempt to make it readable. If there are any mistakes lurking in the text, the fault is entirely mine.

MIDNIGHT'S CHILDREN

Rajiv Gandhi, Narendra Modi

Rajiv Gandhi was born three years (20 August 1944) before Independence of India (15 August 1947), and Narendra Modi was born three years (17 September 1950) after Independence. The two belong to the same generation and, more than metaphorically, to the post-Independence generation. When Gandhi became prime minister of India in tragic circumstances after the assassination of incumbent prime minister and his mother Indira Gandhi on 31 October 1984, he was 40 and he became the first prime minister from the post-Independence generation. He consolidated his position when the elections he had called for in the last week of December 1984 gave his party, the Indian National Congress, a massive mandate of 414 Lok Sabha seats out of 543. How the ambiguous and extraordinary verdict fizzled out in five years' time and how Rajiv Gandhi lost the election in 1989 is an intriguing political story of its own. Thirty years later, in the 2014 Lok Sabha election, India got another post-Independence generation prime minister in Narendra Modi, with a simple majority in the Lok Sabha for his Bharatiya Janata Party (BJP) with 283 seats. In an ironic political twist, Modi seems to pick up the post-Independence generation baton from Gandhi at a time when he is confronting his son, Rahul Gandhi, who was the face of Congress in the 2014 electoral battle. There is the distinct possibility that what had happened to Rajiv Gandhi in 1989 where his Congress was reduced to the single largest party could happen to Modi as well and in the summer of 2019, the BJP could find itself as the single largest party as did Congress 30 years earlier.

The political trajectory of the two leaders was predictable. The seeds of dynastic succession were laid quietly when Rajiv Gandhi stepped into the political shoes of his younger brother, Sanjay Gandhi, who was his mother's close political aide from June 1975 when the Emergency was imposed to his death in an air crash in June 1980. Rajiv Gandhi won the Lok Sabha seat from Amethi, Sanjay's constituency, and he was appointed the general secretary of the party. It was clear ever since Indira Gandhi formed Congress (I) in 1978 after her party's defeat in the 1977 Lok Sabha election post-Emergency that she was the sole authority in the party. Although many senior Congress leaders followed her from the Congress of the 1969–1977 vintage when she led the breakaway group, there were few in the party who could claim to be leaders in the party on their own. Whatever they were in the party was largely due to Indira's approval. The reality was a little more complicated. The power structures and power relations in the Indira-led Congress were not simple monarchical ones. Indira's unquestioned position at the top depended on her ability to win a general election for the party. If she failed to do it, there would be challengers. In 1969, when she broke from the then mainframe Congress party, she was the prime minister. And she was able to draw the middle-rung leaders to her side. In 1978, she depended on Congress leaders Devaraj Urs in Karnataka (then Mysore) and Chenna Reddy in Andhra Pradesh (now divided into Andhra Pradesh and Telangana) to bolster her position. These were the only two states which had voted for Congress in the 1977 election. In 1980, it was the breakaway Congress of 1978 which had romped back to power under Indira. The dynastic dynamics depended on winning general election in the country. So, when the party acquiesced in Rajiv Gandhi being chosen as prime minister by Indira's loyalists in the government immediately after her death, the expectation was that he should run the government and win the election. Rajiv's position was consolidated in the electoral verdict of December 1984.

Narendra Modi's political journey began as that of a Rashtriya Swayamsevak Sangh (RSS) foot soldier, where he had to evade arrest and work underground against the Indira Gandhi government during the Emergency. Modi was not a member of the Bharatiya Jana Sangh (BJS), the precursor of BJP. Modi was inducted into BJP, which was established in April 1980, in the middle of the decade when Rajiv was the prime minister of the country. At the time, Modi could not have imagined that he would be prime minister one day. He was part of then BJP President L.K. Advani's *rath yatra* from Somnath to Ayodhya in 1990, which made Hindutva BJP's political plank. And he was slowly climbing the political ladder in the party. Rajiv Gandhi was the leader of the Opposition at that time. He was assassinated on 21 May 1991 during the Lok Sabha election campaign which was necessitated by the 1989 election result which left no party in the saddle. The Congress party then chose P.V. Narasimha Rao, an about-to-fade-away party leader, as the president of the party, who then became prime minister in June 1991. The trend of 1989 with no party getting a majority on its own continued through the elections of 1996, 1998, 1999, 2004 and 2009. It changed in 2014 with Modi at the helm of BJP.

It also took 30 years for someone from the post-Independence generation to become prime minister. Prime ministers after Rajiv Gandhi—V.P. Singh (born in 1931), Chandra Shekhar (born in 1927), P.V. Narasimha Rao (born in 1921), H.D. Deve Gowda (born in 1933), I.K. Gujral (born in 1919), Atal Bihari Vajpayee (born in 1924) and Manmohan Singh (born in 1932)—were born at least a generation or two before Independence. They led India into the 21st century, the dream of Rajiv Gandhi, with a steady hand indeed, because it would be a sociological fallacy to believe that a large country with a huge population of young people can only be led by a young leader. We will see that Gandhi and Modi have not made a remarkable success of their respective mandates—the mandate was overwhelming in the case of Gandhi more than that of Modi—because of the complexities of the country's political, economic and social structures. As Modi completes his term, it is clear that being young was not enough to govern the country.

Apart from the fact that they belonged to the post-Independence generation, Gandhi and Modi came from the opposite ends of the political spectrum. Gandhi was a political liberal in the general sense of the term, Modi a right-wing nationalist. The two represent the competing political traditions of India and point to the vibrant Indian democracy which has a place for opposed worldviews. The political reality that triggered the massive electoral victory of Congress in December 1984, nearly two months after the assassination of Indira Gandhi on 31 October, had dark shades of nationalist frenzy that one usually associates with the right-wing political ideologies. The election campaign, especially the full-page newspaper advertisements in the pre-24 × 7 TV news channels and Internet era, was loud and ominous. But Rajiv Gandhi seems to have steadied the 'ship of state' by reasserting moderation in tone, and a policy of reconciliation after the election, whether it be in Punjab or Assam, the two major states where violence and parochialism were the dominant notes. There was the dark shadow of mass killings of Sikhs in Delhi in wake of the assassination of Indira Gandhi, and it cast a long shadow on the political vision and career of the young leader which he could not shake off.

Modi trudged the path to the political peak in the hard way, working his way up from the ranks as it were, though it was not always his ability or his understanding that pushed him up. He was a diligent party man who was on guard through all the political highs and lows of the party's political fortunes, and when opportunity came his way, he grabbed it by the forelock. He was not the most qualified man to be made chief minister of Gujarat at the end of 2001 when there was trouble in the BJP government of Chief Minister Keshubhai Patel. L.K. Advani was the man calling the shots in the party at the time, and he had created a ring of middle-rung leaders in the party organization, and there emerged an Advani lobby in the party. Modi was part of Advani's legion. And he was sent to Gujarat as chief minister, though he had never fought an election until then. It was the writ of Advani that was then running in the party. But once he was sent to Gujarat, Modi picked up the reins and proved his abilities as a person who can be ruthless and efficient. But as in the case of the anti-Sikh riots in the three days after Indira Gandhi's assassination, the three days of anti-Muslim rioting in Gujarat in wake of the burning of Sabarmati Express coach carrying Vishva Hindu Parishad (VHP) volunteers, after an altercation at the Godhra station, has remained the albatross around Modi's politics, though he won three state assembly elections—2002, 2007 and 2012—on a trot after that. Rajiv Gandhi barely looked back on the anti-Sikh riots, but Modi carried out an ostensible act of penitence in the form of 'Sadbhavna' fasts in September 2011, and he wrote a little read blog in December 2013 after an Ahmedabad magistrate's court cleared him of charges, where he sought to bare his soul. While Gandhi's political baptism came after he became the prime minister, Modi ran the gauntlet in his years as Gujarat chief minister, when the US government refused to give him a visa in 2005 when he applied for one to address expatriate Indians in New York and Florida. He then addressed them through videoconferencing.

Is there anything distinctive about the emergence of Gandhi and Modi, 30 years apart, as prime ministers from a post-Independent India generation? It is happenstance and nothing more. It was inevitable that sometime or other, a leader from the new generation would be leading the country as the decades roll by. What is of significance and interest is the politics that Gandhi and Modi represented. The supporters of each leader are likely to argue that the two are different from each other as chalk and cheese, which is indeed the case in terms of their individual backgrounds and temperaments. Gandhi belonged to the upper middle class, some would even say aristocratic, and he was a liberal by temperament because he belonged to the social upper crust. Modi, on the other hand, came from a lower middle class, small-town background, schooled in right-wing nationalism born of a resentment that the Hindus—the majority religious group in the country—suffered from political bondage right from the days of Turkish invasions, generally termed Islamic invasions, from 11th century onwards which culminated in the British, Western, Christian rule of about 150 years from the beginning of the 19th century to the middle of the 20th. And the right-wing nationalists nursed fierce resentment against the 'foreigner'. But they were in a hopeless situation because they had absorbed unwittingly and unconsciously as well as by force of circumstances cultural and social mores of the Turks/Muslims and British/Christians, which they could neither reject nor accept. Gandhi never had to face the psychomachia that was the lot of Modi's politics.

In many ways, Gandhi marks the end of the tether of liberal consensus that reigned in post-Independence India from Jawaharlal Nehru, Gandhi's maternal grandfather, to about the 1980s, though Indira Gandhi showed signs of strain in the liberal consensus. She was inward and religious—her close aide and press adviser of some years H.Y. Sharada Prasad called it spiritual—though she was unwavering in her commitment to the pluralist polity that was forged by the founding fathers of the Indian Constitution in 1950.

Rajiv Gandhi was free of the inner pulls that Indira Gandhi might have experienced. He seemed an easy-going humanist, who did not bother too much about inner dilemmas which had no easy answers. But Modi is the perfect foil for Gandhi in terms of attitudes and inner stresses he brings to the political table. Modi's way of working out his and the nation's inner demons is to look to a technological future, where India stands tall in the world with an underpinning of lofty, vague and empty Hindu idealism.

Gandhi and Modi at one level represent change of guard of generations, but it is only on the surface. Beneath the surface, the age-old alienation and antagonism persist which played out in the struggle over reservations in government jobs of Other Backward Classes (OBCs) announced by V.P. Singh, the man who replaced Gandhi as the prime minister in 1989, and which became the Mandal flare-up, with clash between traditional upper castes and the emerging intermediate castes of Hindu society in 1990. BJP, under Modi's mentor Advani, brought to the forefront the issue of constructing a Ram temple in place of Babri Masjid in Ayodhya. It led to rioting in end-1990 and pushed the right-wing Hindu party to national centre stage. Without the Ram temple agitation, BJP would not have become a force to reckon with. It seemed in the 1990s that India had regressed into a proto-medieval cauldron of caste and communal clashes. There were hints of catastrophe and near-apocalypse, but as the century and millennium ended, a kind of political equilibrium was emerging, but this was an uneasy equilibrium where majoritarianism had gained an upper hand and the old comfortable zone of secularism under a liberal dispensation had been relegated into the background.

It turns out that Gandhi and Modi, the torchbearers of a new generation, have been representing two faces of the polity, with Gandhi on the losing side and Modi the victor. But the emergent majoritarianism too may not last, though it is yet to run out of steam. But the weaknesses and the cracks in the new balance of political and cultural currents and counter currents are clearly visible. It is clear that majoritarianism cannot hold India, which is an inherently diverse polity, together. India cannot become an efficient techno-powered economic powerhouse in the manner of post-Second World War Germany and Japan because its soul agonies about culture, faith, social harmony and beliefs have not been sorted out. The Hindu majoritarian solution sought to be imposed by BJP and its ideological mentor, RSS, on the contrary is turning out to be inadequate. The sense of national unity and purpose is missing, and the Modi rhetoric of nationalist glory sounds vainglorious because it lacks inner harmony.

The 30 years that span the emergence of Gandhi in 1984 and Modi in 2014 had not really been a simple journey forward. There were small peaks and small troughs on the way. There was neither untainted glory nor unredeemable tragedy here. The story is complicated, interesting and riveting. It is the story of Independent India struggling to make sense of itself even as it steadily treads the path of economic amelioration. The poverty, famine, malnutrition, disease, illiteracy and bleak backwardness of the 1950s and 1960s are a thing of the past. The economic future, despite the inclement conditions, looks brighter than before. India is poised to become an economic powerhouse if not an economic superpower. But its economic success will not make its politics simple or easy. They become complicated and stressful because India must rediscover its civilizational métier at the intellectual level. To adapt the words that Shakespeare gave to Brutus in the play *Julius Caesar*, India's soul is at war with itself. It cannot become a world leader unless it finds inner tranquillity.

Gandhi and Modi, the parties and the politics they represent, are an external image of the inner uneasiness and turmoil. The 1984–2018 period is a tale of political turmoil and economic achievement. The old truth that man does not live by bread alone is borne out by the state of the nation in these three decades. In our times, politics is the mirror of the heart of the nation. It is tempting to believe that cracks in the mirror give a distorted image of the heart. It looks like that there are cracks in the country's heart as well. How it can be mended is beyond the scope of this book. What this book intends to do is to hold up the mirror and show the cracks, call them fault lines if you will, of the political landscape.

In the mid-1980s, when Gandhi came on the scene, there was the false dawn of a post-ideological world as the Cold War petered out, and the ideological tussle between Western liberal democracy and communism to gain the souls of the newly independent countries in the wake of the Second World War and the liquidation of the European colonial empires became defunct. The new general secretary of the Communist Party of the Soviet Union (CPSU), Mikhail Gorbachev, had started out on his *glasnost* (openness) and *perestroika* (restructuring), loosening Kremlin's iron grip over Russia and the East European communist bloc. United States President Ronald Reagan and British Prime Minister Margaret Thatcher, with their free market worldviews and the determination to roll back the state, were ruling the roost among the Western countries. Communist Party of China Chairman Deng Xiaoping gave the new mantra to China that it did not matter what the colour of the cat was as long as it caught the mice. It was not the fault of Rajiv Gandhi that he felt himself situated in a sweet spot when he talked of India's ancient culture and spiritual values at the welcome ceremony at the White House in July 1985 after Reagan announced the Festival of India in the United States, which was decided upon during Indira Gandhi's visit to Washington in 1982. It looked like Gandhi would lead India into the 21st century and that ideologies and strife can be safely left behind. At home, Gandhi made peace deals in the troubled states in Punjab and Assam, and he broke the ice with China's Deng after 24 years with a long and warm handshake. But the reverie was broken by 1989, when he lost the election, and the country lost its political optimism.

But there was a dark side to the sunny surface of Rajiv's politics. He walked into the maelstrom of the divisive politics of religion, not out of desire and belief but due to compulsions of political expediency. He carried through the Muslim Women (Protection of Rights on Divorce) Act, 1986, to counter the 1985 Supreme Court verdict in the famous Shah Bano case where it ruled that a divorced woman was eligible for alimony under the civil law and she is not bound by the customary Islamic law that governed marriage and divorce. It was clear that Rajiv had no view in the matter and he followed what seemed necessary for Congress to retain its hold in the Muslim community, especially the conservative and reactionary leadership. It was also during this time that his government was compelled to ban Salman Rushdie's controversial novel, *The Satanic Verses*, because one of the firebrand politicians, who was also a retired Indian Foreign Service (IFS) officer, Syed Shahabuddin, had made it into a burning question. The Islamic clerics raised a hullabaloo and the government fearing violence banned the import of the book. While these actions seemed calculated to pacify the vocal, reactionary Muslim leadership, there was a move to handle VHP, a right-wing Hindu organization which was engaged in the agitation to build a Ram temple at the site of the Babri Masjid in Ayodhya, claiming it to be the birthplace of one of the prominent Hindu gods, Rama. Although he had no role in the opening of the locks of the Ram Lalla shrine in the premises of the Babri Masjid in Ayodhya, he started his election campaign from Faizabad, near Ayodhya, in October 1989, and the Congress government in Uttar Pradesh quietly facilitated the foundation-laying ceremony for the temple in Ayodhya in November 1989. There is as yet no clinching evidence as to what prompted Gandhi to take these decisions; the political implications were clear. He ended up stoking the flames of Muslim and Hindu fanaticism, which continue to threaten Indian polity ever since.

It would be easy to blame Gandhi for sacrificing Congress's ideology of secularism—keeping religion and politics separate—for short-term political gains by flirting with the reactionary elements among the Muslims and Hindus. What is of greater importance is the fact that even as India was steadily moving on the path of economic development, an emerging middle class was regressing into religious bigotry. The veneer of secularism, which was the ideological pillar of the Indian republic ever since the Constitution was adopted in 1950, was getting peeled off. For three decades and more after the holocaust of Partition of 1947, which saw the death of thousands of Hindus and Muslims and the migration of millions from the two newborn states of India and Pakistan, religious hatred was a rising its ugly head again. Political leaders like Gandhi flowed with the tide without understanding the underground social rumblings. The paradox of an India that was moving out of poverty and towards prosperity experiencing atavistic religious fury stands in need of explanation. All that social scientists have been able to do is to point an accusing finger at Gandhi for failing to stem the rising tide of hatred, or even for fanning it.

The emergence of Modi in the election of 2014 indicated the triumph of right-wing majoritarianism. Modi also represented the political mood of the world where strong leaders such as Shinzo Abe in Tokyo, Xi Jinping in Beijing, Vladimir Putin in Moscow and Recep Tayyip Erdogan in Ankara held the reins of power, and assertive nationalism became the sign of the times. Majoritarian rule promised political stability. But it is not to be because fluctuations of the fortunes of global markets are seen to rock the economies of countries with strong leaders. Second, there seems to be little space for all the assertive nationalisms because sooner or later they are going to clash with each other in the form of trade wars. US President Donald Trump's trade war of imposing tariffs and raising trade barriers against China is a clear symptom, despite the knee-jerkiness of the decision. Political majoritarianism is too brittle in the face of economic turmoil. National economies cannot hope to notch higher growth rates even as global markets go through economic troughs and highs.

The majoritarian consensus in India under Modi is not standing on firm ground.

Gandhi and Modi cannot claim to be young leaders of a young and modern India. Young and modern have been assumed to be synonymous, and by the extension of the same logic, Gandhi and Modi had to be modern. But the two leaders have ridden to power on the tide of an anti-modern sentiment. Gandhi's massive 1984 mandate was greatly based on a sense of irrational anger among the people in the wake of Indira's assassination. They felt that the nation was under siege. Indira's assassination was the first major political killing after that of Mahatma Gandhi in 1948. The country fell into a tizzy. It was a verdict based on the emotion of fear on a mass scale. Gandhi and Congress played on the sentiment in the 1984 election campaign. Gandhi tried to flex India's muscle in countries such as Maldives and Sri Lanka with the sense that India is a power to reckon with. This was in contrast to Indira Gandhi's candid statement at the welcome ceremony at the White House in 1982 where she said that India had no global interests, though it was interested in global affairs. The woman who intervened and facilitated the birth of Bangladesh in 1971 was brutally pragmatic in 1982. Her young son was carried away by his youthful energy.

Modi's obsession with technology-driven economic growth hides his irrational desire to make India the *Jagatguru* (the world's mentor) in the spiritual sense, hence his sense of happiness when the United Nations agreed to his suggestion of an International Yoga Day. He believes that India will and should conquer the world through its cultural and spiritual values, which is not a realistic and rational ideal. Gandhi believed in the milder version of this cultural conquest of the world, while Modi subscribes to the aggressive variant.

In contrast, the older leaders who served as prime ministers between Gandhi and Modi were realistic and pragmatic. They did not entertain the fancy notions of national glory. They addressed the national challenges of making India a workable democracy with a sustainable rate of economic growth.

II Chapter

ECONOMIC REFORMS

Precursor to Inheritor

There are teasing questions: When did the reforms begin? Who brought them in? Who thought of them? Many have no hesitation in saying that economic reforms began in 1991 and the man who set the ball rolling was Prime Minister P.V. Narasimha Rao. Sanjaya Baru, former media advisor to former Prime Minister Dr Manmohan Singh, and Princeton-trained academic Professor Vinay Sitapati have been pushing the line that Rao is being denied the credit that duly belongs to him, that the reforms revolution is his handiwork and that it is 'evil' Congress, especially the party's ruling family, the Nehru–Gandhis, that is trying to shut out what is essentially a Rao legacy.

As we shall see later in the book, Rao, the Machiavellian politician, did not believe or disbelieve in economic reforms. He implemented them as he found it was necessary to do so. And in 1994, at a party convention, he had no hesitation in declaring that he only implemented the reforms agenda set out in the 1991 Congress manifesto, which was prepared when Rajiv Gandhi was around, and therefore he was only a 'legatee' and not the man who set the reforms agenda. Rao was not a free market ideologue, nor was Dr Singh, who was the finance minister in 1991. Singh crafted the specific policy measures. Rao claimed later in a TV interview with Shekhar Gupta during the 'Walk the Talk' programme that he (Rao) stood like a rock behind him (Singh) in pushing the reforms. But he did not ever declare his faith in a free market economy. Rao had even admitted in a private conversation that the economic reforms had to be done stealthily and that there was no other way of doing it. His public stance was that the

Congress government was not junking the public sector, the pillar of socialist economy, in any way.

The only man who could claim to be a market-oriented reforms evangelist was P. Chidambaram, who served as minister for commerce in Rao's cabinet and when he offered to resign over alleged conflict of interest in Fairfax, an American financial investment concern, Rao displayed his Machiavellian flair and accepted the resignation promptly. But Chidambaram was never in a position to pursue his dream of a market economy, though he did present what was hailed as a 'dream Budget' in 1996 as finance minister in Prime Minister H.D. Deve Gowda's government. But the only ripples that 'dream Budget' caused was an economic nosedive due to market conditions beyond the control of Chidambaram. When Chidambaram returned to Congress and became finance minister in 2004 in the Manmohan Singh government, he was a much-chastened man, and whatever enthusiasm he had for a free market economy was quite muted because Congress, back in power after eight years in opposition, had to pursue populist measures like farm loan waivers.

The thought that India had had enough of socialism and that it needed to turn towards a market economy clearly belongs to Rajiv Gandhi. He was in an advantageous position because he carried no historical baggage despite his maternal grandfather being a believer in some sort of democratic socialism and his mother having flirted with populism for a short while somewhere between 1969 and 1974. We find that the first traces of economic reforms began in 1974 when the then Finance Minister Y.B. Chavan reduced the rate of the top income tax from 97.75 per cent to 77 per cent, though the recommendation of the Direct Taxes Enquiry Committee was to bring down the highest slab to 75 per cent. In 1976, then Finance Minister C. Subramaniam further reduced the highest slab of income tax from 77 per cent to 66 per cent. There was a recognition then that investments in the private sector needed to be incentivized and that capacity expansion was to be encouraged. But there was no talk as yet of taking the economy towards the market. The tendency to encourage private enterprise strengthened further in the second term of Indira Gandhi as prime minister from 1980 to 1984. But there was still no talk of abandoning socialism. Even Rajiv Gandhi repeated the socialist mantra, but he quoted his grandfather to say that socialism is not distribution of poverty but distribution of wealth. And he talked of making the public sector enterprises efficient and competitive, and accountable, by referring to the low rate of return on investment in the public sector. There was a change in both tone and emphasis. The major contribution of Rajiv Gandhi was that he started the dialogue on keeping up with the changing trends in the world economy and pointed to the changes then happening in the Soviet Union and China.

In his reply to the Motion of Thanks to the Address of the President in the Lok Sabha on 22 January 1985, Rajiv Gandhi expressed a radical viewpoint which sounds uncannily 2018-ish: 'Industry is not necessarily the best place for employment. Sometimes it is the most inefficient place for employment. We have to look how we can increase even more than industry can give us.' And he appears to have a realistic and critical view of what the situation is on the ground. He said,

> We cannot pretend to be equal to other countries when we are operating systems which are 10 years or 20 years out of date. The world today is moving very fast and, towards this end, we will introduce a new educational policy which will be targeted at a more modern type of employment.

In the 1990s and at the turn of the century, there was a transformation in the education and employment profiles of at least the urban youth. They were no longer waiting for their turn at the government's employment exchanges, which were conspicuous in the 1960s and had disappeared in the 1990s, but were working at BPOs (business process outsourcing), which became a trend. It gave birth to information technology (IT)-driven services sector from the 1990s into the 2000s. India became the global IT hub, and IT became the engine of India's economic growth.

Narendra Modi has inherited the IT revolution and the economic growth it had triggered. He acknowledged the change that had happened in his first speech as prime minister from the ramparts of Red Fort in New Delhi on 15 August 2014. He said,

> Brothers and sisters, the youth of India has completely transformed the identity of India in the world. Earlier, in what manner did the world know our country? Till only 25–30 years back, if not more, there were many people in the world who thought that India was a country of snake charmers, it was a country which practiced in black magic. The real identity of India had not reached the world, but my dear brothers and sisters, our youngsters, 20–22–23 years old youngsters have mesmerized the whole world with their skills in computers.

And it was based on this achievement that he mooted the idea of Digital India. And he suggested that the youth of India through small and micro enterprises should make all those things which India is importing, and that they should also be able to export these things. He said,

> Brothers and Sisters, I would like to pose a question to my youngsters as to why despite them, we are forced to import even the smallest of things? My country's youth can resolve it, they should conduct research, try to find out as to what type of items are imported by India and then each one should resolve that, through may be micro or small industries only, he would manufacture at least one such item so that we need not import the same in future. We should even advance to a situation wherein we are able to export such items. If each one of our millions of youngsters resolves to manufacture at least one such item, India can become a net exporter of goods.

Modi's vision is simplistic and the idea is clear that India is ready to take off and it is poised to dominate the world economy. The reality, of course, is different. The Indian workforce is not the most skilled across the board, though it is efficient and competitive, in plain words, cheaper, in terms of wages. Lower wages are not exactly a disadvantage as many Asian countries, from Japan to South Korea to the Association of Southeast Asian Nations (ASEAN) Tigers, realized from the 1960s to the mid-1990s, and India and China are realizing it now.

Modi understood that the challenge was to use the IT power of the Indian economy to strengthen the domestic economic and social conditions, and he declared the agenda:

> If our country has this strength, can we think something about the country? Our dream is, therefore, of 'Digital India'. When I talk of 'Digital India', I don't speak of the elite, it is for the poor people. You can imagine what a quality education the children in villages will get, if all the villages of India are connected with Broadband Connectivity and if we are able to give long distance education to the schools in every remote corner of the villages. If we create a network of telemedicine in the places where there is a shortage of doctors, we can have a clear guideline of the way in which health facilities have to be provided to the poor people living in those areas. The citizens of India have mobile phones in their hands, they have mobile connectivity, but can we walk in the direction of mobile governance? We have to move in a direction where every poor person is able to operate his bank account from his mobile, is able to demand various things from the government, can submit applications, can conduct all his business, while on the move, through mobile governance and if this has to be done, we have to move towards 'digital India' and if we have to move towards 'digital India' then we have a dream.

RAJIV'S CAMELOT

Blink of a Dream

Camelot comes with tragic strings. It brings hope and light, but the hope is shattered and the light fades out. For Rajiv Gandhi and his family, it began on a tragic note—the assassination of Indira Gandhi—and it ended seven years later with the assassination of Rajiv Gandhi. There was the poignant moment that photographers snapped at the funeral of Indira Gandhi on 3 November 1984, which showed a bespectacled Rahul Gandhi, then a teenager, hugging his father as the flames engulfed the pyre of his grandmother. Sorrow and innocence were captured in that picture. On 24 May 1991, Rahul, who had just crossed his teen years, was seen walking and even running alongside the cortege of his father, and at the site of the funeral, Sonia Gandhi wearing dark glasses could be seen asking Amitabh Bachchan, a family friend and matinee idol, to get something done. Rajiv's Camelot opened and ended with death.

The three days that followed Indira Gandhi's assassination at the hands of her Sikh bodyguards turned Delhi from a mourning city into a burning capital, where thousands of Sikhs were targeted by mobs; men and boys were stabbed and burned. It was a massacre on a scale that was not seen in Delhi since the days of Partition in 1947. The mayhem in Delhi was so widespread that people did not turn out in large numbers to see the funeral procession of Indira Gandhi. The city was a wreckage. Rajiv Gandhi stood guard by the body of his mother, which was lying in state at Teen Murti Bhavan, the home of the first prime minister, where Indira, Rajiv and his brother Sanjay had spent the years between 1947 and 1964 when Nehru died.

He was sworn in as prime minister by President Zail Singh on the evening of 31 October. Rajiv flew back from Kolkata, then Calcutta, and Singh from Oman, where he was in the middle of a state visit. This was the first time when a son had taken over from his parent as the prime minister of India. It was a dynastic succession within a democratic framework. There is much dark speculation as to how this was done. Rajiv Gandhi had been in politics just for four years. He stepped into politics after the death of his brother, Sanjay, who was a politician, in June 1980, and Rajiv was apolitical. In the four years between the death of his younger brother and that of his mother, Rajiv was still finding his feet in politics. But once he was sworn in as prime minister, Rajiv took to office with poise. He did not seem to be embarrassed that he was stepping into the high office without much quali-fication, and that it violated the democratic spirit. In that moment of national tragedy, it seems that everyone in Congress and in the government was shaken, and they did not have the time to pause and ask the question whether it was right that Rajiv should take over as prime minister in place of his mother.

The only other time a family succession of this kind took place was when Jawaharlal Nehru succeeded his father Motilal Nehru as the president of the Indian National Congress at the Lahore Session in 1929. Interestingly, Motilal wanted Jawaharlal to succeed him and wrote to Mahatma Gandhi that he would want it this way. Motilal conceded in his letter to Mahatma that Sardar Vallabhbhai Patel deserved to be the president after his heroic role in the Bardoli Satyagraha. Gandhi obliged, and Patel had to wait for his turn until the 1931 session in Karachi. The inside story as to what went through Gandhi's mind when he got this letter from Motilal, or whether Jawaharlal was told about the dilemma, or whether Patel had been told the reason why his elevation as president of the Congress is being deferred by a year, remains unknown.

Similarly, how Rajiv's elevation as prime minister had been accomplished remains unclear. P.C. Alexander, who was principal secretary to Indira Gandhi, claims that he had effected the succession after consultation with the senior cabinet members. There is no reason to suspect the veracity of his version as it stands, but it shows the working of the government at the highest level in a bad light. It shows the unbridled power a bureaucrat close to the prime minister wielded in the making of a political decision. Alexander as a bureaucrat should have had no hand at all in the matter. President Zail Singh should have sworn in the most senior cabinet minister as acting prime minister, and he should have waited for the Congress Parliamentary Party (CPP) to elect its leader before he was sworn in as prime minister. It can only be inferred that Indira Gandhi's assassination stuck fear in the heart of the ruling party, and everyone was confounded. It was in this moment of confusion that it clutched at a straw of certainty in choosing the son to replace the slain mother. It was a moment of democratic India's weakness.

Former President Pranab Mukherjee, in his second volume of memoirs, *The Turbulent Years: 1980–1996*, describes vividly how the decision was made, and how a truncated Congress Parliamentary Board (CPB), comprising just him and P.V. Narasimha Rao, as two other members—Kamalapati Tripathi and Maragatham Chandrasekhar—were not in town, passed a resolution nominating Rajiv Gandhi as prime minister, and General Secretary G.K. Moopanar had drafted the letter to President Zail Singh, informing him of the CPB's decision. Mukherjee says that it was decided not to declare the death of Indira Gandhi officially until Rajiv was sworn in as prime minister, and the new government was formed.

He also narrates, quoting Zail Singh's memoirs, that even the president had made up his mind that Rajiv Gandhi should be made the prime minister on his own. Mukherjee says that the common feeling among the senior members of Congress and of the cabinet was that there should not be an interim government, which would be the case if there were to be an acting prime minister, and that this would send out a wrong signal in a fraught situation. So a bunch of leaders, bureaucrats and the president of the country agreed to make the son of the dead prime minister her successor in office. Apart from a sense of panic, the seasoned Congress leaders must have also recognized the advantage of the son of the dead prime minister leading the party into the election, and the tremendous sympathy it would generate among the voters.

The panic and fear among the senior politicians of the ruling party, and the president of the country, do not speak well of a democratic polity. Mukherjee writes that Rajiv Gandhi was sworn in as prime minister at 6:45 PM in the Rashtrapati Bhavan, along with four ministers, P.V. Narasimha Rao, P. Shiv Shankar, Pranab Mukherjee and Buta Singh. Mukherjee says that it was he who had advised Rajiv to include Buta Singh, a Sikh, keeping in mind the sensitive situation.

Despite the justification offered by Mukherjee, the rationale of choosing Rajiv Gandhi to take over as prime minister lacks rationality. The justification—there is one—comes in the massive mandate, with Congress winning 404 of the 514 seats, cornering a share of 49.10 per cent of the votes in the December 1984 Lok Sabha election. The election was due in January 1985.

Rajiv Gandhi was sure why he and his party had won the election, and he declared the reason behind the election verdict of December 1984 when he told the Lok Sabha in his intervention on 22 January 1985: 'We had one issue in front of us—India's unity, integrity, India's nationalism—and this is what has been won in this election.'

At the beginning of 1985, 37-year-old independent India had a young prime minister who was 40, his wife Sonia who was 38, and children Priyanka 15 and Rahul 13. It was a picture-perfect family, and it symbolized young independent India. For a moment, it seemed that India had managed to break free from an oppressive past, both the glory and the abomination. There were dark shadows lurking in the corners. But 1985 was a bright year for India and for Rajiv Gandhi. It seemed that the new prime minister had no historical baggage and that he would look at issues with a fresh outlook and would remain pragmatic.

He was confronted with major problems in Punjab and Assam, which marred the second term of Indira Gandhi in the prime minister's office. And he went about it with both firmness and open-mindedness. He signed an accord with Sant Harchand Singh Longowal, president of the Shiromani Akali Dal (SAD), on 24 July 1985, which comprised 11 points, including a reference to the controversial Anandpur Sahib Resolution, to which the accord said:

> 8. Centre-State relations 1. Shiromani Akali Dal states that the Anandpur Sahib resolution is entirely within the framework of the Indian Constitution, that it attempts to define the concept of centre–state relations in a manner which may bring out the true federal characteristics of our unitary Constitution, and that the purpose of the resolution is to provide greater autonomy to the state with a view to strengthening the unity and integrity of the country since unity in diversity forms the cornerstone of our national entity. 2. In view of the above, the Anandpur Sahib Resolution insofar as it deals with centre–state relations stands referred to the Sarkaria Commission.

The Anandpur Sahib Resolution was the bone of contention between the Akalis and the central government led by Indira Gandhi. Rajiv Gandhi skirted around the issue by restricting its scope to Centre–state relations. Mention of the resolution in the accord was a way of giving in to the stand of the Akali Dal. The accord was a symbolic victory for Rajiv Gandhi, which showed that he was determined to deal with the Punjab problem without prejudice and fear in the wake of his mother's assassination. He also sought to deal with the relatively moderate Akali Dal, whom Indira Gandhi and her Punjab advisers had sought to edge out, which gave rise to extremist elements like Jarnail Singh Bhindranwale. But the accord was sought to be subverted by the extremists in Punjab when Longowal was killed by them on 20 August 1985.

Rajiv Gandhi turned to address the Assam problem. Home Secretary R.D. Pradhan signed an agreement with All Assam

Students Union (AASU) and All Assam Gana Sangram Parishad (AAGSP) on 15 August 1985. The 'Memorandum of Settlement' is about the 'Foreigner Problem Issue', and it refers to the consultations between the central government and the Assam groups from 1980 onwards. It notes:

1. Government have all along been most anxious to find a satisfactory solution to the problem of Foreigners in Assam. The All Assam Students' Union (AASU) and the All Assam Gana Sangram Parishad (AAGSP) have also expressed their keenness to find a solution. 2. The AASU through their Memorandum dated 2nd February, 1980 presented to the Late Prime Minister Smt. Indira Gandhi, conveyed their profound sense of apprehensions regarding the continuing influx of foreign nationals into Assam and fear about adverse effects upon the political, social, cultural and economic life of the State. 3. Being fully alive to the genuine apprehensions of the people of Assam, the then Prime Minister initiated the dialogue with the AASU/AAGSP. Subsequently, talks were held at the Prime Minister's and Home Minister's levels during the period 1980–83. Several rounds of informal talks were held during 1984. Formal discussions were resumed in March 1985.

One of the key elements of the Assam Accord is the cut-off date:

Foreigners Issue 5. (1) For purpose of detection and deletion of foreigners, 1-1-1966 shall be the base date and year. (2) All persons who came to Assam prior to 1-1-1966, including those amongst them whose names appeared on the electoral roles used in 1967 elections shall be regularized. (3) Foreigners who came to Assam after 1-1-1966 (inclusive) and up to 24th March 1971 shall be detected in accordance with the provisions of the Foreigners Act, 1946 and the Foreigners (Tribunals) Order, 1939. (4) Names of foreigners so detected will be deleted from the electoral rolls in force. Such persons will be required to register themselves before the Registration

Officers of the respective districts in accordance with the provisions of the Registration of Foreigners Act 1939 and Registration of Foreigners Rules, 1939. (5) For this purpose, Government of India will undertake suitable strengthening of the governmental machinery. (6) On the expiry of the period of ten year following date of detection, the names of all such persons which have been deleted from the electoral rolls will be restored. (7) All persons who were expelled earlier, but have since entered illegally into Assam, shall be expelled. (8) Foreigners who came to Assam on or after March 25, 1971 shall continue to be detected, deleted and expelled in accordance with law. Immediate and practical steps shall be taken to expel such foreigners. (9) The Government will give due consideration to certain difficulties expressed by the AASU/AAGSP regarding the implementation of the illegal Migrants (Determination by Tribunals) Act, 1983.

There is then a difference between the Rajiv–Longowal Accord and the Assam Accord. In the accord with Longowal, Rajiv Gandhi had to pull back in the Akali Dal those who were marginalized. There is, on the other hand, continuity in the Assam talks. The Memorandum of Settlement or Mizo Accord was signed with the Mizo National Front (MNF) leader Laldenga, ending a 20-year insurgency, on 30 June 1986 in dramatic circumstances. Rajiv Gandhi wanted Home Secretary R.D. Pradhan, who conducted year-long negotiations with Laldenga, to sign the accord before he retired on 30 June. The accord was signed at 9:00 PM after the law secretary clarified that Pradhan would retire only at midnight because he had not handed over charge!

One of the interesting points in the Mizoram Accord was the provision not to impose any central legislation with regard to local laws and customs unless the Mizoram Assembly decides on it. It says,

Notwithstanding anything contained in the Constitution, no act of Parliament in respect of (a) Religion or Social practices of the Mizos, (b) Mizo customary law or procedure,

(c) Administration of Criminal or Civil Justice involving decisions according to customary Mizo Law, (d) Ownership or transfer of land, shall apply to the state of Mizoram unless the Legislative Assembly of Mizoram by resolution so decides.

But there was the caveat: 'Provided that nothing in this Clause shall apply to any Central Act in force in Mizoram immediately before the appointed day.'

Assembly elections were held in Assam and Punjab. The newly formed Asom Gana Parishad (AGP), which was led by student leaders from AASU and AAGSP, came to power, and young Prafulla Mahanta, one of the student leaders, became chief minister. In Punjab, the Akali Dal came to power, with the mild-mannered Surjit Singh Barnala taking over as chief minister. Laldenga headed the interim government in Mizoram, and it was accorded statehood on 7 August 1986. For the moment, hope shone bright on the horizon.

In Parliament, Gandhi dusted off an old anti-defection bill and got it passed in January 1985 itself. And he claimed rightly in the Lok Sabha on 30 January 1985:

> Mr Speaker, Sir, this Anti-Defection Bill has been pending for a long time. I think it was first mentioned almost seven years ago. We have taken it up as one of our first major tasks because we felt that this is an area where public life needs cleaning up.... We also have promised that we will carry the opposition with us. And I am happy to say, Sir, that we carried almost all of the opposition.

The Bill was passed with 398 ayes and 2 noes. Senior Opposition leader Madhu Dandavate told Speaker Balram Jakhar to make it a unanimous vote.

It was also the year that young Gandhi jetted to major world capitals and let it be known that India has a young leader with new ideas. As he told the US Congress in his speech on 13 June 1985, 'India is an old country, but a young nation, and like the young everywhere, we are impatient.' And this was followed by his Dr Martin Luther King Jr-like declaration of a dream: 'I am young and I have a dream. I dream of an India—strong, self-reliant, and in the front rank of the nations of the world and in the service of mankind.' The idealistic tone got frayed in the following years. He was trapped in realpolitik. But 1985 was a good year for him and for India. It was also the year that India unveiled its soft power through the Festival of India in Paris and in Washington. And Rajiv Gandhi struck a rapport with the 74-year-old genial American President Ronald Reagan. They 'hit it off' with each other.

The year closed for Rajiv Gandhi on a reflective note, which came through in his famous speech at the Congress Centenary session on 28 December in then Bombay (now Mumbai). What stood out was his comment that Congress had been reduced to a party of power brokers. What was overlooked was the confession about his entry into politics, his political apprenticeship. It was a moment of rare candour. He said:

> When I started my political work, it was only with the motive of being by the side of my mother. She bore with stoic fortitude the irreparable loss of a son who had been a tower of strength. She gave me no direction, no formulae, no prescriptions. She just said, 'Understand the real India, its people, its problems.' So I plunged into work.

He said that he travelled extensively for two years, met people, read and reflected. And he felt that though much was accomplished, much more could have been done. He held himself back from declaring his impressions: 'I kept my counsel to myself, as I was an apprentice in the great school of politics.' When he went back to his mother and spoke to her, she was assured that he had got a sense of India, and she shared her dreams and apprehensions about India.

RAJIV'S FALL
Furies Unleashed

Trouble began for Rajiv Gandhi and his government early in 1986, just a year into office. The elation of an exhilarating electoral victory did not last long. The first defensive step that the Rajiv government took was the introduction of the Muslim Women (Protection of Rights on Divorce) Bill, 1986, on 25 February 1986. Law Minister A.K. Sen told the Lok Sabha while introducing the Bill,

> Our understanding is that the features of the Bill reflect the opinion of the vast majority of the Muslims about their own law. It is quite true that about hundred or five hundred intellectuals or quite a large number of people outside that particular list feel in a different way. That must be so in a democratic country when each one is entitled to interpret his own religion including the Quran. But we have to find the consensus of the community, and we have found it in a particular manner. We do not think we have found it wrongly.

Sen was diffident and apologetic throughout. He did not say whether the new Bill would be fair to the divorced woman and her financial plight. He stuck to the very narrow view as to what the Muslims had to say about the issue, and how it is necessary for the government and for the society to see to it that Muslim law is adhered to. He said,

> We are on a limited field of divorce of women and their provision for maintenance during various periods of their life and certain contingencies which may arise, that is, when during these periods those who are charged with

the duty to maintain them fail to do so, the community has to take charge. That is according to our understanding of the Muslim law. This may be different from views of the Supreme Court. We are not going into the merits. As quoted by the Supreme Court, as Aayat 241 of 'Surah Baquar' only says, that it is the duty of the virtuous men to maintain the indigent divorced women. Now, virtuous men means according to the Muslim Scholars the community and not the husband of the divorced woman. Her maintenance is a charge on the community as a whole. Therefore, we have provided that under circumstances the duty to maintain indigent divorced women is on those certain members of her family and failing them on the community.

He outlined the different stages through which the husband has to maintain his divorced wife—the *iddat* (waiting) period, if she is bearing his child and for two years when she is suckling his child, and at the end of it, Sen said in a tone of helplessness: 'Now, what are we to do? Are we not to follow the injunction of the Muslim law on this matter? I am afraid we have to.'

The government faltered.

More than three years later, intervening in a debate in the Lok Sabha on the communal situation in the context of the proposed *shilanyas* by VHP on 10 November 1989, Minister of State for Home Affairs P. Chidambaram offered yet another weak defence. Speaking in the debate on 12 October 1989, he said,

The first issue which inflamed the communal passions was the controversy over the Muslim Personal Law. But I believe the Government resolved to the satisfaction of the Muslim community. The CPI (M) Politburo in its resolution which was quoted by Mr Shahabuddin in his magazine accused the Government of appeasement of Muslim fundamentalists when we took that step. Nevertheless, Government took that step because Government thought it was a right step and it was necessary to communal harmony and peace.

Intervening in the Lok Sabha on 11 October 1989, Home Minister Buta Singh, responding to the comment of Indian Union of Muslim League (IUML) member G.M. Banatwala that the government is facilitating the shilanyas, said,

> I have explained to Shri Shahabuddinji and his colleagues. Soon after I came back from Lucknow, I explained to them that this is what we have tried to do to avoid confrontation in every village in every street (interruptions).... The Government authorities will see to it that no confrontation is built up.... Only a few bricks will come and at the predetermined place by the District authorities, the bricks will be collected there. Over the question of shilanyas, it is baseless to say that the Government has given any land. I repudiate it. No Government land has been given. If they do it in some of their temples, how can I prevent it? (interruptions) After a detailed discussion, I explained to him (Shahabuddin) the arrangement which the Vishwa Hindu Parishad for the first time has given in writing that they abide by the court verdict. I do not know what else you want. After that, Mr Shahabuddin has gone on record to say that this is the step in the right direction... (interruptions)

Intervening in the same debate on 12 October, Chidambaram said, 'We have gone through a three-year period of what I would call, competitive religiosity that added an acute dimension to the practice and profession of religion.'

The Rajiv government was caught on the wrong foot between two fundamentalisms—Muslim and Hindu—and on both occasions, the government fell back on legalities.

There was a certain cavalier attitude in the government about the military and how they could make use of it. Rajiv Gandhi and his relatively young companions in the government seemed to be a little unhinged by the armed might of India which was at their command. This was indeed the attitude in what went into Operation Brasstacks of November 1986–March 1987. Chief of Army Staff General Krishnaswamy Sunderji and Minister of State for Defence Arun Singh, who was also a school fellow of the prime minister, planned a military exercise, which is the norm of armies in peace time, in Rajasthan near Pakistan border. It was in a way an act of preening, a very immature thing for a national army to indulge in.

It reached a flashpoint in January 1987. The rationale of the exercise apparently was to test the induction of the new mechanized divisions and new communications systems that were inducted into the Army, which is a normal paradigm of all military exercises. But in January, Pakistan upped the ante and considered the massing of the Indian troops in the Thar Desert in Rajasthan, where the exercise was taking place, to be a prelude to outbreak of war. A similar military exercise was underway on the Pakistani side and after the end of the exercise, the troop formations did not disperse. This was seen on the Indian side as a provocative build-up on the part of Pakistan.

Rajiv Gandhi appeared bewildered. And this was shown in his actions. On 20 January, he remarked at a press conference that there would be a new foreign secretary when the serving Foreign Secretary A.P. Venkateswaran was present and he was conducting talks with his Pakistan counterpart. Second, V.P. Singh, who was finance minister until then, was made the defence minister. There was a flurry of diplomatic activity on all sides before it became clear that there was no need for apprehension on the Pakistani side, and that war was only a rumour because of lack of communication, military and diplomatic, on both sides. In March 1987, Pakistani nuclear scientist A.Q. Khan told Indian journalist Kuldip Nayar that Pakistan possessed a nuclear bomb. This was a bizarre episode, which pushed the frayed India–Pakistan relations into a tizzy.

It did not, however, inhibit the use of Army in operations in Sri Lanka towards end-1987 as a peace-keeping force, officially called the Indian Peace Keeping Force (IPKF), deployed in the

Tamil-majority northern and eastern areas of the island as a follow-up to the Sri Lankan President J.R. Jayewardene and Rajiv Gandhi in Colombo in July 1987. It proved to be a misadventure when the Indian force got involved in fighting the Liberation Tigers of Tamil Eelam (LTTE), restoring law and order and facilitating provincial elections. The government of prime minister Ranasinghe Premadasa government left it to the Indian Army to do the difficult job of managing an insurgency-affected region, abandoning its own responsibility. It was not the job of the Indian Army, but it was trapped into carrying out the task. It was done at a great cost. The Indian Army lost 1,200 men, and it was this which led to the assassination of Rajiv Gandhi in May 1991. Analysts have offered many reasons for the military debacle, but that did not prevent the Rajiv Gandhi government from responding a year later, in November 1988, to send Indian paratroopers to Maldives at the request of President Abdul Gayoom to abort a furtive coup led by a bunch of Sri Lankan militants. The Indian force successfully handled it with aplomb. India had emerged as a regional power, and it seemed that it would be forced to engage in difficult, and sometimes unsuccessful, strategic operations.

The issue that haunted Rajiv Gandhi through his term in office broke out on 17 April 1987 when the Indian papers carried a report based on a broadcast of Swedish radio that arms manufacturer Bofors had paid bribes to Indian politicians and defence officials to sell the 155 mm towed howitzers in March 1986. Defence Minister K.C. Pant made a statement in the Lok Sabha on 20 April 1987: 'On the eve of the finalization of the contract, in response to a reiteration of Government's Policy and a demand for confirmation, vide their letter of 10th March 1986, that they did not employ any Representative/Agent in India for the project.' What infuriated the Opposition was the statement issued by Defence Ministry which not only denied the charge of bribes being paid but also described the Swedish radio report as an attempt to destabilize the country. Rajiv Gandhi asked the Opposition for proof about payments. But as the controversy dragged on, the government went on the defensive. It had to admit that payments were made by Bofors to three companies. The Opposition and the media went into overkill to claim that Rajiv Gandhi and people close to him were the recipients of ₹640 million or SEK319.4 million kickbacks.

Chidambaram introduced the Anti-Defamation Bill in the Lok Sabha on 29 August 1988, which proposed

> to make publication of imputations falsely alleging commission of offences, by any person as an offence. Those who make such imputations do so just for the sake of calling into question the reputation of the person concerned. Often they do not have any intention of pursuing the matter any further with the appropriate authorities.

He tried to assure:

> Apprehensions voiced by the hon. Members that any novel or unusual provisions are there in this Bill are totally unfounded. The Bill faithfully follows the existing provisions of the Indian Penal Code. The Bill re-introduces provisions which were introduced in 1978 by the then Government in the form of Indian Penal Code (Amendment) Bill 1978 which was passed by the Rajya Sabha and which lapsed in the Lok Sabha on its dissolution.

E. Ayyappu Reddy, a Telugu Desam Party (TDP) member, confronted Chidambaram:

> But there is a new chapter added—Chapter II. Criminal imputation is made an offence. Mere criminal imputation is made an offence? (interruptions) Even in your elaborate speech, or even in your brief speech, you have not referred that the previous amendment contained this or that the Law Commission has made a recommendation to make criminal imputation an offence. This is a new offence. Have you studied the implications of this new offence?

Amal Datta, a Communist Party of India (Marxist) (CPI(M)) member, was more direct in his criticism. He saw the connection between the Bill and the Bofors controversy. He pointed out:

> This is definitely a Bill to suppress any kind of criticism of the Government by the critics, by the Press and even by the Opposition. We will not be able to speak; even we will not be able to speak if the elections come; we will not be able to ask, 'Who took the money in the Bofors deal?' Everybody knows that in the Bofors deal money has been paid; the JPC has also said that ₹ 64 crores have been paid.

He said that allegations of wrongdoing against those in the government could not be proved because people had no access to the official documents. He said,

> In all developed Parliamentary democracies and in other democracies in other countries, there are Acts which allow citizens and the press to get information from the Government which they think is necessary for the public. These are in the form of right to information Acts which have been passed in U.K., U.S.A. and other places. If such an Act is there, then, in the event of there being a suspicion or a rumour, we can have this satisfied by asking the Government to disclose the information relevant to this kind of accusation or allegation or rumour.

Chidambaram was forced on the back foot, and he tried to wriggle out of the tight spot. His counterargument was as follows:

> Sir, the two journalists who investigated Watergate—and I am sure you have read their book on how the investigation took place—did so with a tremendous sense of responsibility. At every stage they would check back with the White House and ask the White House if the White House had any comments to make. At every stage he would go back to what was described in the book as deep-throat, verified and then only published. That is why I say this and I

maintain this. I maintain the statement I made earlier. I disagree totally with Chitra Subramaniam's conclusion. I think her inferences are wrong, her efforts are praiseworthy but her inferences are wrong. The analysis which they seek to make is commendable. But the conclusions are totally misconceived. But knowing that paper, I am willing to make a statement that nothing which Ms Chitra Subramaniam has written amounts to a false allegation or a false imputation of a criminal offence against any person. That is the high standard which the paper has so far maintained although its conclusions are something which I totally disagree. But how many maintain that standard?

P. Chidambaram, intervening in the discussion on Bofors based on the Comptroller and Auditor General (CAG) Report on the Defence Services in the Lok Sabha on 25 July 1989, said,

> Sir, the fact that certain amounts were paid by Bofors to three companies—for brevity I call them Svenska, A E Services and Pitco—is a fact which was admitted by Bofors, firstly before the Government of India and later formally before the JPC (Joint Parliamentary Committee). Those payments have been described in various terms but I do not propose to enter into those controversies.

He would not, however, agree with the CAG observation that

> Although the Ministry had decided in May 1985 that procurement of imported weapons and equipment would be made directly from the manufacturers and agents eliminated, it did not obtain a categorical assurance from Bofors in regard to the engagement of agents. According to the findings of the Joint Committee of Parliament, Bofors paid SEK 319.4 million to three companies not domiciled in India. In the absence of a suitable provision in the contract to exclude agents, no reduction in cost to the extent of payments made to the agents could be sought by the Ministry from Bofors.

Chidambaram argued,

> There are many significant statements in this paragraph. Firstly, even the Comptroller & Auditor General does not wish to enter into a controversy about the nature of payments. He describes them as payments, a very neutral word and even he does not try to characterize these payments as a bribe or as a kickback or a commission and, I would say quite rightly, because he had no evidence before him to do so.

What Chidambaram objected to is the observation of the CAG that no written assurance was given by Bofors and that there was no 'suitable provision in the contract' about excluding agents. He said that the CAG was going beyond his remit, and that Attorney General (K. Parasaran) told the Joint Parliamentary Committee (JPC) that an oral commitment was a sufficient commitment.

The Sri Lankan military intervention cost Rajiv Gandhi his life in May 1991 at a time when it appeared that he would make it back to power in the Lok Sabha elections that were underway at the time, and the Bofors deal of 1985–1987 cost him the election in the winter of 1989.

Despite being under attack at every turn from 1986 onwards, Rajiv Gandhi tried to press on with what he wanted to do. Even as late as 15 May 1989, he was arguing forcefully and persuasively about the 64th Constitution Amendment Bill which would make periodic elections to Panchayati Raj institutions mandatory. He argued how this would deepen democracy and shared his vision of democratic devolution, which was idealistic. He said that superstructure of Indian democracy was strong, but the foundation was weak. His argument was as follows: 'Putting together both Houses of Parliament and all the State Legislatures, we have only about five thousand to six thousand persons representing a population of 800 million.' He felt that the proportion of elected representatives to the electorate was much too small. And that elections to Panchayati Raj institutions would increase the numbers of elected representatives to 0.7 million. 'The people's stake in democracy will be increased by a factor of 115,' he said. And he expressed concern over the fact: 'There is a second deleterious consequence of the vast chasm that separates the general body of the electorate from the small number of its elected representatives. This gap has been occupied by the power-brokers, the middle-man, the vested interests.'

More importantly, he envisioned an exalted role for the panchayats in the planning process:

First is the power and authority of the Panchayats to draw up plans within the framework of guidelines and conditions to be stipulated by the State Governments. These plans will constitute the basic inputs for the planning process at higher levels. Thus, we will ensure that the voice of the people, their felt needs, we must put an end to planning from above. We must put an end to priorities being conceived and decided at ethereal heights far removed from the realities on the ground. We must put an end [to] paternalistic planning. We must initiate a process of people's planning.

In the same rhetorical vein, he outlined what the panchayats would be entrusted to do:

The proposed Eleventh Schedule seeks to vest in the Panchayats the major responsibility for the administration of poverty alleviation programmes. It would entrust panchayats with education and culture as well as health and family welfare, women and child development. We propose to request the State Legislatures to make social welfare programmes for all the weaker and handicapped sections, a functional responsibility of the Panchayats. We also propose to give to the Panchayats the responsibility for the public distribution system, which is so crucial for the survival of weakest and the poorest as also for the general health of the rural economy.

The political imagination of Rajiv Gandhi seems to have played with the double idea of a Gandhian nation of village republics and a nation state that will play an important role in the world, with its economic and technological power, with its military power, with its cultural power and with its message of peace as represented by Mahatma Gandhi. He was lost in a hazy vision of the unrivalled glory of India, the weakness of all modern Indians. And this was indeed the final note of his term in office. In the valedictory address to the last session of the Lok Sabha on 13 October 1989, he made a curious connection between the end of the Cold War and the Gandhian message. It was a strange kind of sentimentalism that, somehow, the world was heeding India's, Mahatma Gandhi's, message. It was expressed in a measured, even subdued, tone. But it reflected blurred thinking. He said:

> If I am asked about the one achievement that this Parliament has had, I could say that even more than removing poverty, even more than passing Bills which will give powers in the hands of our people to remove corruption and power-brokers and various sources of exploitation that takes place, even more than many Bills that we have passed to strengthen women, the Bills that we have passed to bring about major changes in our electoral processes, strengthen our democracy, there are so many that Parliament has done, I would say the first big achievement of this Parliament is in bringing the ethos of Indian civilization across the globe and having it accepted by a very large number of people even in countries that did not believe in what stood for. Our struggle is not just a struggle for removing poverty and exploitation within India; our struggle is to remove poverty and exploitation across the globe. And during these years we have brought about a change in global thinking. For the first time, there is a break-up of the power blocs. There is a new international democracy that is coming out of the old system. I do not want to take credit for this. The credit must go to Gandhiji who raised his voice, to Panditji who showed the

way, to Shastriji and Indiraji who sat in this seat and guided us in that direction. We have only followed in their footsteps and we have been able to walk a little further because they had guided us so far.

In this final speech in the Lok Sabha as prime minister meanders, he was lost for words and ideas. He looked a man who was at the end of his political tether but who was not aware of it.

Prime Minister Rajiv Gandhi's story is incomplete without V.P. Singh, his finance minister in 1985 and 1986, his defence minister in 1987, and the man who quietly crossed swords with the head of the government. There seemed to be a clash of worldviews which was not apparent in the beginning, but which emerged gradually. While Rajiv Gandhi had definitive views about 'power brokers', V.P. Singh quite early made up his mind that big industrialists who were illegally stashing money in foreign banks should be tracked down. And as finance minister, he was in the right position to do so. Apart from carrying out income tax raids against big industrial houses, including that of the Kirloskars, he had allowed his ministry officials, Bhure Lal and Vinod Pande, to hire an American detective agency to help track the foreign bank accounts and investments of India's business houses which were evading taxes at home. When equations turned sour between Rajiv Gandhi and V.P. Singh and he resigned, a commission of two Supreme Court judges, M.P. Thakkar and S. Natarajan, was appointed in early 1987 to enquire whether the hiring of a foreign detective agency endangered national security. The commission's report was laid on the table of Parliament and it was discussed at length in December 1987. The Opposition refused to accept the validity of the report because it saw it as an attempt to put V.P. Singh in the dock at a time when Rajiv Gandhi was in the line of fire over the Bofors deal.

During a discussion on the Bofors issue in the Lok Sabha on 15 November 1988, Madhu Dandavate made a prescient statement, a year ahead of the defeat of Rajiv Gandhi's government in the election and the emergence of V.P. Singh. He said,

They may try to attack Vishwanath Pratap Singh but I shall conclude by saying the manner in which he conducted himself when Bofors episode took place, when he was on the Treasury Benches and when he quit the Treasury Benches and joined the Opposition, his behaviour has been exemplary, moral and ethical. And so long as these standards are maintained in the country, men like V.P. Singh will be able to mobilise public opinion in the country. Once it is mobilized, there will be no other alternative for the Prime Minister but to quit his post, go and seek the mandate of the people and get rejected by the people. That will be the fate that the Prime Minister will have to meet. I am sure this will happen, Sir.

Singh became the prime minister and he replaced Rajiv Gandhi in 1989 as Dandavate had predicted. But Singh did not get the mandate. His Janata Dal won 164 seats to Congress's 197. Rajiv Gandhi had lost the commanding majority he had won in 1984, but he remained the leader of the largest single party. Singh had to seek the support of BJP and of the Left parties to form the National Front government. It was a rickety government, and it fell in November 1990, after 11 unstable months in power.

Singh was a 'pure' politician. He had no ideological roots, and whatever he did was dictated by exigency and expediency. He did not display ambition, nor did he show any drive for power, but he worked in such a way that others were forced to accept his leadership. He checkmated Rajiv Gandhi while he was in government and forced the prime minister to push him out. He became a martyr of a corrupt Congress's intolerant ways. When he came into office, he did not show the puritan's zeal for rooting out corruption. He was quite adept in making symbolic gestures like his announcement that he would implement the Mandal Commission report recommendation of 27 per cent reservation for OBCs in government jobs at a time when there were not too many government jobs in the first place. He tried his best to manage the political contradictions pulling his government apart and made the pseudo-Chanakyan pronouncement that politics is the art of the possible, which reflected more political aesthetics rather than realpolitik. He was not ruthless enough, and he was only too ready to throw in the proverbial towel.

He acted without motive and purpose when he was in the Rajiv Gandhi government, and he did the same when he became prime minister. And, ironically, he changed Indian politics forever without meaning to do so. His sole contribution was to have pushed Rajiv Gandhi and Congress off centre stage. No member of Nehru–Gandhi family has managed to become prime minister since then. And Congress has not recovered its centre of gravity as it were. He spent his post-prime ministerial years pursuing poetry and painting, offering acute political analysis, but he had no over-arching vision for the country. Singh resembled Wajid Ali Shah, the indolent and aesthetic Nawab of Lucknow, who presided over a decadent polity in 19th-century India. Singh was a quintessential Gangetic plains politician who came on the stage and played a cameo role at a time when the Hindi heartland was caught in caste and religious fervour.

V Chapter

THE TRAUMATIC TURN

Rajiv Gandhi was assassinated on the night of 21 May 1991 at Sriperumbudur, near Chennai. It was a searing moment as the country was in the middle of the Lok Sabha election. The human bomb, Dhanu, who had explosives tied to her in a belt, stood there waiting with a garland in her hand at the election meeting, and as Rajiv Gandhi walked towards her on the way up to the dais, Dhanu offered him the garland and bent, triggering the explosion. There was chaos near the dais as blood-spattered bodies were lying all round.

Wife Sonia Gandhi and daughter Priyanka flew to Chennai and brought the body to Delhi in a special flight. The blanched face of Sonia Gandhi showed the sorrow that struck her like lightning as she walked behind the coffin down the steps of the plane and Priyanka walked behind holding her on the morning of 22 May.

The Congress Working Committee (CWC) met on 22 May, chaired by P.V. Narasimha Rao. The meeting was attended by 12 of the 18 committee members. Among those who were at the meeting were K. Karunakaran, Arjun Singh, H.K.L. Bhagat, Ghulam Nabi Azad, Meira Kumar, Balram Jakhar, Jagannath Pahadia, Rajendra Kumari Bajpai and party treasurer Sitaram Kesri. The special invitees were Pranab Mukherjee, Jitendra Prasad, M.L. Fotedar, P. Shiv Shankar, Maharashtra Chief Minister Sharad Pawar and Andhra Pradesh Chief Minister N. Janardhana Reddy.

The committee, after the customary two-minute silence in honour of the dead leader, appealed to the people to show restraint and ensure peace and harmony. Arjun Singh then proposed Sonia Gandhi as president of the party. The party note says that everyone present supported, and she was elected Congress president. It was also decided to send a five-member delegation led by Rao to meet President R. Venkataraman and explain the situation arising out of the assassination.

The committee met again on 29 May, and it was presided over by Bhagat in his capacity as general secretary All India Congress Committee (AICC) in charge of Working Committee affairs. The committee approved its proceedings of 22 May. Sonia Gandhi turned down the offer to be president, but she urged the party to elect the leader unanimously. Arjun Singh proposed Narasimha Rao to be Congress president and Ghulam Nabi Azad seconded. Rao was elected president unanimously.

Rao in his acceptance speech said,

> I am grateful to the Congress Working Committee for electing me as President of the Indian National Congress. At this moment surcharged with grief and gratitude, my short response would be: I shall do my best, let us get on with the job together. I am sure this is what the people want, what the thousands upon thousands of Congress workers want.

He concluded saying,

> The Indian National Congress has shown that its ideological and institutional strength can lift it from the grief of the deepest tragedy to meet the greatest of challenge. Today it feels proud of the example of Mrs Sonia Gandhi, and the personal courage she has shown in this tragedy, as well as her deep commitment to the future of her Congress Party and her India. We are grateful to Soniaji.

The committee, in a special resolution, expressed its gratitude to Sonia Gandhi, recording its

> deep appreciation of the manner in which Mrs Sonia Gandhi responded to the request for taking over the reins of the party. Even though she has declined our request, the sentiments expressed by her are heart-warming and

give inspiration to all the Congress-I men who look forward to her for constant guidance and concern so that we will be able to discharge our duties in a manner that our beloved leader, Mr Rajiv Gandhi, would have liked us to do.

Narasimha Rao was elected provisional president, and the party note says, 'Some admirers of Mrs Sonia Gandhi continued to demand that she be persuaded to accept the office of party president.'

Congress had to quickly gather itself in the face of the tragic blow. It did. Congress emerged as the single largest party with 243 seats. It was a minority government.

VI
Chapter

ENDING THE FREE FALL

Big changes do not really happen with a big bang. So it had been with the economic reforms. The apparently revolutionary economic reforms were stated in an almost bureaucratic language in the speech that President R. Venkataraman delivered on 11 July 1991, the first day that the new Parliament met after the Lok Sabha election, and it showed surprising clarity on what the new government intended to do.

The Rao government declared in the President's address:

> Government recognises that the country is in the midst of an economic crisis. It has been living beyond its means and adopting soft options. We have been overtaken by events. We must act now. No sacrifice is too great to safeguard our economic independence and the country must prepare itself to take hard and unpleasant economic decisions.

Was there an economic crisis that proclaimed deluge, apocalypse or just total breakdown? The figures do not indicate that India had hit the rock bottom, at least internally. The president's speech notes that industrial growth was at 8.4 per cent in 1990–1991 'compared to 8.5 per cent during the 7th Plan period'. The food grain production for 1990–1991 was projected to be 177.2 million tonnes. And the speech refers to the unprecedented success: 'This will be the third successive year of increased food grains production and this has happened for the first time since independence.'

In reply to a question in Lok Sabha on 12 July tabled by Congress members, Pawan Kumar Bansal and V. Srinivasa Prasad, Minister of State for Finance Rameshwar Thakur presented the economic indicators. They showed that GDP growth, which was at 10.4 per cent in 1988–1989, had fallen to 5.2 per cent in 1989–1990 and to 5 per cent in 1990–1991. Agriculture growth was at 4.5 per cent in 1990–1991, which was up from 1.7 per cent in 1989–1990. Industry grew at 8.7 per cent in 1988–1989 and 8.6 per cent in 1989–1990. Exports rose from 29.1 per cent in 1988–1989 to 36.8 per cent in 1989–1990 and fell sharply—by more than half—to 17.5 per cent. But imports in 1990–1091 were at 21.9 per cent, and compared to the exports figure it does not really look so disastrous. The imports clocked 26.9 per cent in 1988–1989 and fell slightly to 25.4 per cent in 1989–1990.

The inflation rates were high but not catastrophically high. The Wholesale Price Index for 1988–1989 was at 5.7 per cent, for 1989–1990 at 9.1 per cent and for 1990–1991 at a sharp high of 12.1 per cent. The Consumer Price Index was 8.5 per cent in 1988–1989, 6.6 per cent in 1989–1990 and again a very high 13.6 per cent in 1990–1991. The fiscal deficit was not too disastrous. It was 7.8 per cent in 1988–1989, 8.0 per cent in 1989–1990 and 8.4 per cent in 1990–1991.

The figures for foreign reserve currency were as follows: ₹66.05 billion in 1988–1989, ₹57.87 billion in 1989–1990 and ₹43.88 billion in 1990–1991.

The figures show that there was economic trouble, but it was not something that could not have been overcome. It seems that the reforms were done not because there was no way out but because the party in government felt the need to change gears and look for a new path. The process began in the 1980s, and the changes that were made in 1990–1991 under the pretext of economic crisis, which was shown as a breakdown, were in many ways a continuation of the path that was followed in a way through the 1980s. The argument given that reforms were adopted to avert economic breakdown appears less convincing. The breakdown has, however, been presented as a fact.

The perfect emblem of the breakdown seemed to be the lease—a technical term for pawning—on 16 May 1991 of 20 metric tonnes of gold through the State Bank of India, which fetched, Thakur told the House in reply to a question, 'foreign exchange of the order of $200 million'. He also informed, 'The period of lease is six months extendable by mutual agreement. The consideration for lease is ₹25 lakh.'

A surprisingly feisty and combative Manmohan Singh, who was appointed finance minister, intervened to explain the lease of gold:

> But when we have no reserves, when exports are down, when Non-Resident Indians are no longer sending money but instead are taking their money out, there was no other option. It pained me greatly and I knew it pained the then Prime Minister. But in that situation there was no other option.

Chandra Shekhar was the caretaker prime minister, and Singh was his financial advisor.

Singh did not end there. He took the argument forward in an aggressive manner. He said, 'Sir, the honourable Member wanted to know the precise value of Government stock. I have the figure with me. I am very pleased to give that figure. It is $200.4 million. That was the value of the gold sold.'

And he went on to explain in the same angry tone:

> Now why are we here? Our party was in opposition. In January, 1990 there was a change of Government. In January, 1990 there was no lack of confidence about our country. Our country was considered creditworthy. There was a positive net inflow on account of non-resident Indian remittances. There was positive inflow of foreign commercial loans. Our economy was considered highly credit worthy. But then something happened.

And the unnamed honourable member asked: 'What has happened?'

Singh answered and in full measure: 'Well, the type of budget that was presented, the loan waiver scheme that was launched which eroded India's credit worthiness, which destroyed India's banking system.'

And like an ace parliamentarian—he had entered Parliament for the first time and this was his second day—Singh took the bull by the horns as it were and plunged into an argument:

> Mr. Speaker Sir, I seek your protection. I have something to say. We are being accused of going to the IMF. But this House should know that the Government in power from January–December went to the IMF twice and they took large amounts of money from the IMF. In spite of that the things they have done weakened our credit-worthiness abroad. Now, it is our responsibility.

What the Rao government addressed was not the immediate economic crisis because the remedy set out in the 11 July President's address was a thorough change in ideas and mindset. But the theme of crisis was emphasized: 'Fiscal imbalances continue to be a major concern for the Government. Despite attempt at controlling expenditure and raising additional revenues the revised estimate of budget deficit for 1990–91 is ₹10,772 crores against the budget estimate of ₹7,206 crore.' And the assurance was given: 'Government is committed to observing strict fiscal discipline.' And there followed the non sequitur: 'The generation of black money will be checked.'

The President's address referred to the balance of payments problem, which was shown as being at the root of the economic crisis:

> The balance of payments position, already under severe strain, was further exacerbated by the Gulf crisis, the direct adverse impact of which is $2.7 billion (over ₹4,900 crores). Of this the additional cost of oil imports alone accounted for $2 billion, while the rest was, among others owing to the loss of exports, evacuation of Indian nationals and reduced inflow of capital. The balance of payments situation has become critical as the flow of funds

from international capital markets did not materialise as anticipated though several countries did offer help.

It was clear that there was a slight sleight of hand there. What the government thought was the reason for economic crisis was given in the 11 July President's address. Singh in his intervention on 12 July blamed the Budget of January 1990 for the problems of the Indian economy in 1991. Singh was hitting back politically and defending Congress, a party which he had joined just a few weeks earlier.

The view about where the economy and the country were to go was not tied up to the immediate crisis. There was a long-term perspective there, and what was brought to the table was a new set of ideas. The President's address then set out the new ideas:

> It is hoped that export trade will get out of the circle of low growth, high cost and stifling controls and once again get on to a high trajectory of growth. Government's ultimate goal is to eliminate all licensing control on the import of capital goods and raw materials except for a small negative list.

And there was the broader and deeper fundamental view of economic principle which had less to do with the crisis. It was about regulation and controls: 'Government will work for extensive deregulation and reduction of bureaucratic intervention. To this end, a comprehensive review of policies and procedures has been initiated.'

What was proposed was a root-and-branch change in the structure of the economy: 'In order to raise the competitiveness and quality of Indian industry to global levels, technology imports will be liberalised and facilitated in areas where Indian technology does not measure up to international standards.'

And there was the third element of investment: 'Changes in procedures are being worked out so that the investment climate is made more conducive for participation by foreign companies and non-resident Indians.'

The other basic aspect of the Indian economy was the public sector, and the new philosophy towards the public sector was set out in the President's address:

> Reforms in the functioning of the public sector are being formulated to improve its performance. The management of the public sector will be strengthened through selection of the best talent available. Public sector managers will be allowed greater autonomy without diluting accountability. A policy is being evolved for disinvestment including workers' participation in equity and for vacating areas of activity where public sector involvement is not essential and where private and joint sectors have developed capabilities.

This statement of the government through the President's address of 11 July was followed by Manmohan Singh's first Budget presented on 24 July. Singh paid tribute to Rajiv Gandhi at the very beginning of the speech:

> Sir, I rise to present the budget for 1991–92. As I rise, I am overpowered by a strange feeling of loneliness. I miss a handsome, smiling face listening intently to the Budget Speech. Shri Rajiv Gandhi is no more. But his dream lives on; his dream of ushering India into the 21st century; his dream of a strong, united, technologically sophisticated but humane India. I dedicate this budget to his inspiring memory.

Singh did not beat about the bush. He went straight to the issues that he saw as wrong and which he proposed to set right. 'The origins of the problem are traceable to large and persistent macro-economic imbalances and the low productivity of investment, in particular the poor rates of return on past investments,' he said. He did not stop there but spelled out his diagnosis of the economic ailment affecting the country:

> There has been an unsustainable increase in Government expenditure. Budgetary subsidies, with questionable social

and economic impact, have been allowed to grow to an alarming extent. The tax system still has many loopholes. It lacks transparency so that it is not easy to assess the social and economic impact of various concessions built into its structure. The public sector has not been managed in a manner so as to generate investible surpluses. The excessive and often indiscriminate protection provided to industry has weakened the incentive to develop a vibrant export sector.

He virtually attacked every aspect of the economy as it existed and found it wanting in all the crucial aspects. It was only after making the general assessment that he summed up the immediate causes of the crisis crushing the economy: 'The balance of payment has lurched from one liquidity crisis to another since December 1990. The current level of foreign exchange reserves in the range of ₹2,500 crores would suffice to finance imports for a mere fortnight.'

And he announced the major changes that were being effected in the economy. He said that important changes in 'industrial policy' had been announced to increase competition between firms in the domestic economy and that this competitiveness would serve as an incentive 'to raise productivity, improving efficiency and reducing costs'.

Announcing changes in the import–export policy which reduced import licensing and encouraged export promotion, Singh did not shy away from attacking one of the cardinal principles of the Indian economic thinking in the political and governmental sphere. He said, 'The past four decades have witnessed import substitution which has not always been efficient and has sometimes been indiscriminate.' And he offered the remedy: 'The time has come to expose Indian industry to competition from abroad in a phased manner.'

The other major reform measure was allowing foreign direct investment in 'specified high-priority industries'. Prompt approval was to be given for 51 per cent foreign equity 'if equity inflows are sufficient to finance the import of capital goods at the stage of investment and if dividends are balanced by export earnings over a period of time'. He also allowed foreign equity up to 51 per cent for trading companies 'engaged in export activities'. And he announced the setting up of a special board which would negotiate with international firms and 'approve direct foreign investment in select areas'. His hope was that this would attract substantial investment that would give 'access to high technology and to world markets'. The prescription was again preceded by plain talk:

> After four decades of planning for industrialisation, we have now reached a stage of development where we should welcome, rather than fear, foreign investment. Our entrepreneurs are second to none. Our industry has come of age. Direct foreign investment would provide access to capital, technology and markets. It would expose our industrial sector to competition from abroad in a phased manner.

The last major policy change that Singh announced in his first Budget was disinvestment, through the offer of 20 per cent government equity 'in selected public sector undertakings' to mutual funds and investment institutions in the public sector and to workers in these firms. Those public sector firms which were sick and there was no way of turning them round were to be referred to the Board for Industrial and Financial Reconstruction (BIFR). And he once again stated the problem and how he planned to tackle it: 'At this critical juncture, it has therefore become necessary to take effective measures so as to make the public sector an engine of growth rather than an absorber of national savings.'

On 29 February 1992, Singh was back with the annual Budget for 1992–1993. He announced, 'Overall, I expect GDP growth in 1991–92 to be around 2.5 per cent, I expect a distinct improvement in 1992–93 and a return to high growth in 1993–94.' He said that it would take 'at least three years' for the economy to get back to 'a path of rapid and sustainable growth'. And he preached the gospel of austerity as a precondition for recovery and growth. He warned: 'Given our limited resources, our people cannot afford to copy the soulless consumerism and the wasteful lifestyles of the affluent countries of the West. Conspicuous consumption has to be actively discouraged. The virtues of thrift have to be emphasised.'

Singh was stung the most by the *Indian Express* report by Bharat Bhushan that the Budget proposals were shown to the International Monetary Fund (IMF) and the World Bank (WB) officials in New Delhi before the Budget was presented to Parliament. Singh went out of his way to explain his views and the government's position. Singh held forth on the issue and argued:

> It has been alleged by some people that the reform programme has been dictated by the IMF and the World Bank. We are founder members of these two institutions and it is our right to borrow from them when we need assistance in support of our programmes. As lenders, they are required to satisfy themselves about our capacity to repay loans and this is where conditionality comes into picture.

He conceded that there were conditionalities and the government had accepted them while defending the decision:

> However, I wish to state categorically that the conditions we have accepted reflect no more than the implementation of the reform programme as outlined in my letters of intent sent to the IMF and the World Bank and are wholly consistent with our national interests. The bulk of the reform programme is based on the election manifesto of our Party. There is no question of the Government ever compromising our national interests, not to speak of our sovereignty.

He turned conspicuously vocal, defending the idea of letting in foreign investment:

> Concern is sometimes expressed that the policy of welcoming foreign investment will hurt Indian industry and may jeopardise our sovereignty. These fears are misplaced. We must not remain permanent captives of a

fear of the East India Company, as if nothing has changed in the past 300 years.

Reforms were not brought in stealthily as it seemed and as it was argued by experts and some pro-reforms Congress politicians. Singh was very clear in his mind, and he argued his case consistently in Parliament. His statements seem to have been ignored at the time they were made or they were dismissed as weak rationalizations. In retrospect, they assume greater gravity than when they were made.

But Rajiv Gandhi in his 1987 Budget speech was hanging on to the ideas and principles of socialism as India's economic goal. He quoted his grandfather Jawaharlal Nehru's speech while introducing the Second Five-Year Plan: 'We have, therefore, to lay great stress on equality, on the removal of disparities; and it has to be remembered always that socialism is not the spreading out of poverty. The essential thing is there should be wealth and production....' And Rajiv Gandhi ended on a careful note, where he does seem to have had second thoughts about socialism but he was not yet willing to abandon it as yet: 'I am committed to planning for socialism in India, socialism which fits in with our genius but nevertheless socialism in its basic meaning of removing disparities and providing equality of opportunity.' Rajiv Gandhi was fine-tuning the definition and meaning of socialism in the same way that his liberal grandfather did. He would speak out boldly the revision of his ideas about socialism in the party forum the following year.

It is, however, hard not to miss the irony in the fact that in the Budget speeches of 1988 and 1989, the finance ministers continued to harp on self-reliance and on the public sector while making significant announcements which were nothing but reforms measures. (There were three finance ministers from 1987 to 1989: Rajiv Gandhi served as finance minister in 1987, Narayan Datt Tiwari in 1988 and S.B. Chavan in 1989.) Tiwari in his Budget speech of 29 February 1988 noted that industrial growth was above 8 per cent 'for four successive years since 1984–85'. And citing the improvements in the rates of growth in power, railways and coal, he went on to say, 'Government attaches the highest importance to building a strong and vibrant public sector.'

But Tiwari, time and again, harked back to Rajiv Gandhi's Budget speech of 1987. He referred to the setting up of the National Housing Bank with an initial capital of ₹1 billion, and announced that the bank 'will become operational shortly'. The more interesting reference was to the developments in the capital market. 'The capital market is an important source for mobilisation of savings for industry and Government have taken several steps to strengthen it.' And he referred to Rajiv Gandhi's announcements the previous year:

> Last year, the Prime Minister announced the decision to set up a separate Board for the regulation and development of the Stock Exchanges. Necessary legislation in this regard is under preparation and the Board is expected to become operational soon. Measures have also been taken to set up Mutual Funds, lay down ground rules for orderly operations of the Stock Exchanges, improve their infrastructure, facilitate share transfers and enforce better discipline on companies entering the market.

The curious, and even radical decision, in retrospect, was the government's decision to allow 'Venture Capital Companies or Funds to invest in new companies in anticipation of future-capital gains.' And the government decided to give 'concessional treatment of capital gains available to non-corporate entities'. And Tiwari anchored the decision on venture capital in solid reasoning: 'We have one of the largest pools of scientific and technical manpower. Yet many of our young and new entrepreneurs find it difficult to raise equity capital because of the risk involved.' It was for this reason that there was need for venture capital funds. And in 1989, Chavan in his Budget speech said, 'The average growth rate of GDP in the first four years of the Plan will exceed the Plan target of 5 per cent,' and said that despite the drought of 1988, the food grain production would be more than the targeted 166 million tonnes, though it was 138 million tonnes in 1988 despite drought.

There were then clear stirrings of reforms in the decisions announced in the Budgets of 1987, 1988 and 1989. Rao and Singh were not really starting from the scratch. The ground was prepared for major economic policy shifts. And the thinking had changed too. Tiwari was a proclaimed socialist and Chavan was a pragmatic Congressman who toed the party line. In 1988 and 1989, the economy was in good shape and the prospects were promising. The perceived crisis and the breakdown of 1991 were as much rhetorical as real.

VII

Chapter

WINDS OF CHANGE

The plan for change has been spelled out. The crisis of 1991 served as a perfect pretext to push for radical change. This was a change that could not have been thought over and worked out in a few weeks' time. It had been then on the anvil for quite some time. It was an invisible change that took place through the 1980s. It did not happen suddenly, out of the blue, in 1991. It is a good signpost. It did not come out of nowhere.

Congress was thinking in terms of reforms in a more systematic manner before P.V. Narasimha Rao took the helm of party and government and before Manmohan Singh was inducted as finance minister. In the manifesto for the 1991 election, the Congress party laid out the ground plan for the shift in thinking about the economy, without abandoning some of the populist underpinnings like poverty alleviation.

The 1980s was the Congress decade, with Indira Gandhi returning to power in January 1980 and Rajiv Gandhi being defeated in November 1989. The 1980s served as a stepping stone for the reforms of the 1990s. In 1980, Indira Gandhi was not the same leader who was a firebrand populist of 1969–1971 vintage. In 1980, India borrowed $5 billion from IMF under conditionalities which remained secret. When N. Ram, then Washington correspondent of the *Hindu*, got the document detailing the conditionalities, there was political storm over the secrecy. Indira Gandhi ignored the criticism and managed to repay the loan before it was due. The move away from official socialism began then, though she would still keep the populist card alive with the 'loan melas' that the Minister of State for Banks, Janardhana Poojary disbursed with vigorous fiscal imprudence. Ironically, in the middle and late 1990s, the banks were chasing urban middle classes to use credit cards, first introduced in the country by Citibank, and an aggressive sales pitch to take loans for buying cars and houses. As the earlier 'loan melas' of the 1980s created non-performing assets (NPAs) for the banks, the end of the 1990s saw the middle classes caught in a debt trap. It was not too widespread and it did not last too long. But there was a glimpse of the abyss of rising debt.

The change in the political mood was ushered in by loud criticism that came from formerly Third World-friendly economist and Nobel laureate Gunnar Myrdal. While receiving the Jawaharlal Nehru Award for International Understanding in 1982, he echoed the Western opinion that aid being given to the Third World was not reaching the poor but it was lining the pockets of unscrupulous political elites in these countries. The old rhetoric of neocolonialism that Ghanaian leader Kwame Nkrumah coined and that Indira Gandhi borrowed began to sound shallow. There were winds of change blowing through Asia and Africa.

The 1991 Congress party manifesto says:

> Poverty alleviation was the central priority of the Indira Gandhi and Rajiv Gandhi governments. More investments were made in poverty alleviation schemes than ever before. Several new schemes were implemented. The proportion of our population below the poverty line was halved from over 51% at the time Indiraji returned to office in January 1980 to an all-time low of 25% by the time Shri Rajiv Gandhi demitted office in November, 1989.

Under the heading 'Industrial Growth', it states:

> India's industrial growth achieved a record increase, touching 12% per annum at its height. This was the result of the major policy initiatives taken during the Seventh Five Year Plan aimed at increasing productivity, reducing costs and improving quality. The accent was on opening the domestic market to increased competition and readying our industry to stand on its own in the face of international competition.

It was not just that the domestic market was opened up. The manifesto delineates that changes were made in the way public sector functioned as well:

> The public sector was freed of a number of bureaucratic constraints and given a larger measure of autonomy than ever before. The technological and managerial modernisation of industry was pursued as the key instrument for increasing productivity and improving our competitiveness in the world. It was a period of visualising new horizons.

The manifesto is a clear declaration that Congress was moving in a new direction, that this new direction was chartered during the 1980s and that in 1991 Congress was promising that it intended to take forward economic modernization, which is liberalization and reforms though the two words are not used, and globalization was clearly implied because there was talk of international competition.

It was not a smooth transition. There was unease in the late 1980s about the change in the direction of the Indian economy, especially after the Bofors story broke out in April 1987. The Swedish radio had run a story that the field gun manufacturer had paid kickbacks amounting to ₹0.64 billion to individuals in high places in the political sphere. The media and the Opposition suspected that someone close to Rajiv Gandhi was paid the kickbacks. The prime minister was under attack. The party reacted. At the CWC meeting on 18 April 1987, the committee adopted a resolution, which stated:

> When Shri Rajiv Gandhi assumed the leadership of the nation, a propaganda offensive was launched that the Jawaharlal Nehru–Indira Gandhi framework of independent foreign policy will be subordinated to the geopolitical necessities and requirements of neo-imperialism and neo-colonialism. A false theory was put forth that modernisation meant submission to the current economic and social doctrines in powerful industrial countries of

the West. The vast Indian market with its tremendous potential for growth was seen as a play-ground for multi-nationals.

And here comes the defence of Rajiv Gandhi:

> Rude shock and disappointment awaited those who had nursed these illusions in the company of their domestic servitors. The Prime Minister, Shri Rajiv Gandhi, did not do any of the things he was supposed to do in the script drawn up in countries that seek to impose their diktat on the developing world.

And at the CWC meeting of 22 June 1987, it was decided to review the socio-economic policies, and there was criticism that liberalization of 'imports of non-essential goods, open invitation to multi-nationals to come and operate in India, dilution of FERA and MTRP had given the impression that the Government was veering towards the right and moving away from socialism'. It was also pointed out that the impression was gaining ground that the government's economic measures were intended to benefit the rich and the poor were neglected.

The committee had also noted that the working class was getting alienated from the party because of the closure of factories 'in the name of modernisation', that the farmers and landless labour were getting estranged because surplus land was not distributed among the landless and that there was no 'worthwhile expansion of small scale industries in the rural areas' as a result of which unemployment had 'reached unprecedented levels'.

There was the warning: 'Unless these policies were corrected and programmes initiated to benefit the poor, landless and unemployed and the shelter-less it would not be possible to arrest the gradual erosion of the party's popularity with the masses.'

The party note says that

> [Rajiv Gandhi] is understood to have justified some of the economic policies, including the liberalisation measures,

initiated by his Government after due thought in order to hasten the pace of industrialisation, to make consumer goods available in plenty and at cheaper prices and also to create avenues for greater employment.

He expressed his willingness to get the policies reviewed 'to find out if any imbalances had crept in or whether the implementation was faulty'.

The CWC met again on 22 July 1987, and it endorsed the expulsion of V.P. Singh and three others from the party, a decision taken by Party President Rajiv Gandhi. The members had even said that they should have been expelled earlier. The party's response to the challenge to V.P. Singh's rebellion and the outbreak of the Bofors story was for the committee to adopt 'for the left of the centre socio-economic policies'.

Significantly, V.N. Gadgil chose the moment to announce the revival of the Congress Socialist Forum, which was started by Gulzarilal Nanda and K.D. Malviya in the 1960s, which criticized 'the economic policies pursued by the government', and Gadgil said that there was no mention of corruption because 'in the context of a discussion of the decadence of capitalist system itself corruption was a non-issue'.

Rajiv Gandhi did not abandon his ideas in the face of the crisis created by the Bofors scandal. And in his inaugural speech at the AICC session at Kamarajanagar near Madras on 23–24 April 1988, he defended the new policies and explained their rationale, showing that the old commitments to socialism had to be redefined in the face of the new reality. This was the theme that Narasimha Rao took up in his presidential address at the party's plenary session at Tirupati in April 1992.

Rajiv Gandhi harked back to the Avadi session of the party in 1955, where the socialist pattern of society was declared as the means to achieve national goals of development and self-reliance. 'The Avadi resolution of 1955 set the Congress party on the path of socialism and self-reliance. It conferred on the public sector the central role in our economic development. It was the foundation of the Industrial Policy Resolution of 1956 at which Panditji explained at Avadi, "We must produce wealth and then divide it equitably. Our economic policy must, therefore, aim at plenty."'

Rajiv Gandhi took pains to argue the need to change in the face of an altered reality. Using almost communist party dialectic, he said,

> The direction set out at in the Avadi resolution is our direction today. But just as Panditji applied these basic principles to the objective conditions of his day, so we must today. Concepts such as these are not dry or static. They are living ideas which emerge stronger the better-rooted they are in reality.

He accepted the fact that India had a powerful public sector with 'a total investment of more than ₹80,000 crore' and that it occupied the commanding heights of the economy. Then he introduced the problem with the public sector: 'But the return of this massive investment is inadequate.' Then he extended his argument as to the changes that needed to be introduced: 'We need to look afresh at how we do things. We are working on ways to improve the return on investment and make much more efficient use of our resources.' He mentioned the three phrases which were reiterated time and again by the Narasimha Rao government: 'We must raise productivity, reduce costs and improve quality.' And the theme of competition found its place as well: 'We must make our public sector, indeed our entire domestic economy, much more competitive.'

And the most clear-cut affirmation of the liberalization policy that Rajiv Gandhi followed and which was under attack came in this speech: 'We are looking afresh at the entire system of controls and regulations. What is needed will be retained, and what is not needed must be discarded. There is no place in a dynamic economy for obstacles to quick decision-making and effective management.'

There was once again the confidence that India faced new challenges and that it could meet them:

As our economy grows in size, sophistication and capability, we must move to take our rightful place in the global economy. Self-reliance today means building the capacity for agricultural and industrial growth, using technology and resources which are in our control. We are confident that we can meet the world economy on our own terms. We should not be afraid to experiment as long as we preserve our national independence.

And he reminded the party about the changes happening in other countries wedded to socialism: 'Countries such as the Soviet Union and China, far more cautious than us, are experimenting with new concepts, putting into practice ideas which only five years ago would have been considered heretical. They are adapting to changes.'

He saw continuity in the new policies that his government was pursuing:

Our economy has done well precisely because we have adapted to the evolving changes of development. The process was begun by Indiraji. We have accelerated the process—we shall persist with innovative change. At the same time we shall remain faithful to our basic principles.

And he struck the note of warning: 'There is nothing in any ideology which says that adaptation and change are regressive. On the contrary, it is only those who are confident that can step out boldly and make their mark. We cannot be left behind.'

Rajiv Gandhi faced opposition from within the party, and the opposition grew vocal because of the political situation created by V.P. Singh's rebellion and the Bofors story with the charge that there were kickbacks to middlemen in the deal for the 155 mm howitzer field gun. This came to a head in 1987 and in 1988. Rajiv Gandhi's speech of April 1988 shows that he was defending his policies. It was not the Opposition that was criticizing him. It was his own party that was attacking him for the liberalization policies. The Opposition, with the defector V.P. Singh in its ranks, helped by a vocal and hysterical media, wanted to target Rajiv Gandhi for his alleged corruption in the howitzer gun deal.

It was not, however, easy for Narasimha Rao and Manmohan Singh to push through the new policies. There was anger and discontent in the party over the devaluation of the rupee and the pledging of gold. At the CWC meeting on 23 July 1991, Singh was made to explain the rationale of the 'drastic decisions' taken. The party note about the meeting says,

> The CWC expressed full satisfaction with the economic policy measures and felt these reflected the thrust of the party's election manifesto after hearing the Finance Minister Manmohan Singh's point of view and clarification. Perhaps for the first time the Working Committee called the Finance Minister to satisfy it why he had taken drastic economic steps. Also, this was the first time when the Finance Minister was made to explain all this at the party's highest policy-making body on the eve of the general Budget.

The note also says, 'Many party leaders in Parliament had openly launched a signature campaign against Dr Manmohan Singh recently. And one Rajya Sabha member, Dr Ratnakar Pandey, had demanded in the House that the Government should change the Finance Minister.'

Facing stringent criticism that he had betrayed the Congress of old, of socialism, of public sector, Narasimha Rao in his Congress presidential address at the plenary session held at Tirupati from 14 to 16 April 1992 referred back to the manifesto and said that the reforms that were being initiated were really the implementation of the promises made in the manifesto. Rao said in his speech of 16 April:

> In the past ten months our Government has initiated far-reaching fiscal and financial reforms. This was done in conformity with our Election Manifesto of 1991 which gives

the main features of the reforms. It is remarkable that even when the Congress was in opposition, the late Shri Rajiv Gandhi anticipated the economic crisis that was coming and incorporated clear and concrete remedial as well as positive measures in the Manifesto.

In the 10,000-word speech, which the party press note says the members heard with attention, Rao argued his case on the basis of logic and reason. On the question of self-reliance, he took his critics head on. He denied that his government had abandoned the idea of self-reliance. 'This is not true', he said, and explained the need to change and to redefine self-reliance. He said,

> Our concept of self-reliance so far has included an emphasis on building up basic industries within the country and on import substitution. The priority given to basic industries was one of the great contributions of Nehru. It is this which has led us to the point today where we are able to consider other options with confidence.

He pointed out that this was not enough and there was need to change and he hit hard at the old idea:

> We believe, however, that the stage has now come when we could review our strategy. Import substitution cannot be an end in itself. The very level of development we have reached has made us independent of the world economy in some respects, but more dependent on it in others. This is an important aspect of the complexity of modern development.

He explained in a simple language the rationale of international trade to the party members:

> There is hardly any country in the world, howsoever developed, which insists on making everything it needs. Not that it does not possess the capacity to do so, but it finds it more economical, in its circumstances, to buy a number of things from others who make them.

And he reached to the new idea of self-reliance after noting that in certain areas, self-reliance remains crucial in the sense that you cannot depend for them on other countries. In other cases, the principle of business had to be as follows:

> The criterion of self-reliance today has to be not whether you can make whatever you need, but whether you can pay for whatever you need. One way of describing self-reliance would be to say that we should be indebted only to the extent we have the capacity to repay.

He extended the same argument to the issue of foreign capital, saying that at one stage native capital had to be protected but that after four decades of independence, 'Our indigenous capital has reached a stage where it can stand on its own feet.' It is just that native capital had become mature. He also said that it was not sufficient: 'But the limitations of native capital, both quantitative and technological, pointed to the need of opening up the economy to external replenishment.' He also issued the general warning that India could not remain isolated, that it had to integrate with the global economy. At the same time, he explained that the public sector was not being dismantled. He underlined the need for creating the public sector:

> It came into existence at a most crucial time in the country's economic history when no one from abroad was ready to help India in the infra-structure area. The public sector therefore stands as a symbol of the country's self-reliance. It was the corner stone of Panditji's vision. It has served the country very well and will no doubt continue to do so. There are those who complain that we are pulling the public sector down. Let me straight-away clarify that we are doing no such thing. Here also what we are doing is to redefine the role of the public sector.

Narasimha Rao explained the new position, the new policies and the need to go with them. He did not succeed in convincing the party and the people of the country. He lost the 1996 election. It will be a matter of debate and dispute whether this was because of the economic reforms he pursued or because he was involved in corruption charges and the discontent in the party was growing, as the government seemed to be inactive and not in command of the situation. At one level, he and Manmohan Singh took shelter behind the fact that the economic crisis inherited from the previous Chandra Shekhar government made change necessary and even 'inexorable'. Narasimha Rao was being both prudent and pragmatic in pushing for the new economic policy.

AYODHYA AGONY

The Ayodhya trouble was brewing menacingly nearly six months before the actual eruption on 6 December 1992. The CWC meetings held at Prime Minister Rao's official residence from July 1992 onwards indicate that the party was watching closely the Ayodhya developments. At the CWC meeting of 21 July,

> The committee discussed the situation arising out of the VHP's Kar Seva for construction of Ram temple at the disputed site in Ayodhya. The failure of the UP Government in implementing the order of the Allahabad High Court to stop the construction work was viewed with concern.

And the party note about it says,

> Some members were of the view that the Congress Government at the Centre must take strong action and maintain its secular image. This is a message that must go to the people and communal forces must be put in the wrong. It was pointed that the Congress also in its Election Manifesto has promised to construct the temple without demolishing the Babri Masjid. This promise should be made known to the people.

It was left to the prime minister to decide about the nature and time of action. There was the caution that government should wait until the Supreme Court verdict was delivered.

On 18 November 1992, in an informal meeting, CWC took note of the 'threat given by Vishwa Hindu Parishad to resume kar seva on 6th December 1992 to build the Ram temple'.

On 3 December, Home Minister S.B. Chavan made a detailed statement in the Lok Sabha, which was followed by a discussion on the tense situation in Ayodhya. Chavan revealed the efforts made by the government to resolve the contentious issue. Chavan told the Lok Sabha that the talks went into the phase of final negotiations, and the prime minister held two meetings with VHP and the All India Babri Masjid Action Committee (AIBMAC) on 3 October and on 16 October. A third was announced for 8 November, but before the third meeting, VHP had announced the resumption of *kar seva* (voluntary service) for 6 December.

Chavan said that a National Integration Council (NIC) meeting was convened on 23 November, and 'after considering all aspects of the Babri Masjid–Ram Janmabhoomi dispute and the report of the Government, the Council extends it wholehearted support and cooperation in whatever step the Prime Minister considers essential in upholding the Constitution and the rule of law, and in implementing the Court's orders.' Chavan noted, 'Unfortunately both the BJP and the VHP abstained from the meeting.'

Chavan, in his statement, also narrated the hearings in the Supreme Court about the issue: On 20 November, the court asked the Union government to state its stance so that the court could issue a suitable order based on the government's stance so that the court's order would be implemented. On 23 November, the solicitor general told the court:

The Government of India is prepared to give to the State Government whatever assistance is required in further-ance of the directions of the Honourable Court; and (b) The Government of India also assured the Honourable Court that the Government will take such action as may be directed by the Honourable Court to secure the enforcement of the order.

On the same day, the court asked the Uttar Pradesh government what assurance it could give that the court's orders would not be violated on 6 December. In an affidavit filed on 25 November, the Uttar Pradesh government sought a week's time to negotiate with the representatives of VHP and the Dharma Sansad. The court gave time until 27 November. The court said that if the state government did not respond and if it failed to convince that the court's orders would not be violated, then it would have to issue the relief that had been asked for, that is, appoint a receiver or issue orders to the central government that the court's orders would be obeyed.

Chavan told the House that on 27 November, the Uttar Pradesh government in its affidavit told the court that it would prevent the violation of the court's orders and that it had a positive response in its negotiations with the various parties connected with the proposed kar seva. The state government also requested to direct the Lucknow Bench of the Allahabad High Court to expeditiously dispose the 'land acquisition case'. Chavan said that the court adjourned the case to 28 November and instructed the state government to 'file an affidavit giving, inter alia, an assurance that no construction material or machinery will be allowed into site and no permanent or temporary structure in violation of the Court's orders would be erected'.

On 24 November, the Union government moved paramilitary troops to Uttar Pradesh to be on hand if the Uttar Pradesh government needed them, and the state government was informed of this movement.

In the debate that followed Chavan's statement, Ram Vilas Paswan alerted that there were already 40,000 *kar sevaks* (volunteers) in Ayodhya. Paswan also pointed out as dangerous the statement made by BJP leader L.K. Advani that people would follow the Dharma Sansad and not Parliament. More than the others who took part in the debate, Paswan saw the dangers and the long-term implications of the communal frenzy that was rocking Ayodhya. He dismissed Chavan's statement as a 'news bulletin'. And he made the acute observation:

> Today the Muslims of the country are a frustrated and a dejected lot. They have a pain in their heart. Try to understand the pain of those who believe in secularism. You may demolish one mosque and the Muslims may not react to it just to protect their own life and property but

the wound as a result of that, will it strengthen the integrity of the country? Do not let them suffer this wound....

And he sarcastically remarked,

> We are happy that the majority of the Congress men feel that the Constitution should be protected and safeguarded, but the Prime Minister may be having some other opinion. When the BJP admires the hon. Prime Minister of the country then it becomes clear that there is something wrong in it. Therefore, those who are in Congress Party should ponder over it.

Turning to senior Congress leader Sharad Pawar, he asked him not to sit silently but speak out, and quoted the lines of Hindi poet Dinkar: '*samar sesh hai/vyadh jo tatasth hai/samay likhega/unke bhi apradh* (The battle remains/Futile to remain neutral/Time will write/Their [those who remained silent] crime)'.

Then he pointed to the real weakness of the government's stance:

> Mr Speaker, Sir, through you I would like to urge the hon. Home Minister not to defer every issue on the plea that the matter is sub judice. The Government is throwing the ball in the court so that it is not blamed. If something happens, it will say that it was the court which did so. One should have a political will.

Indrajit Gupta of the Communist Party of India (CPI) warned that in a tense situation, even a small incident could provoke trouble that could lead to violence and loss of lives and property. It was noticed by the other Opposition members that BJP's leaders L.K. Advani and Murli Manohar Joshi were already absent from the House. Atal Bihari Vajpayee, speaking during the debate, admitted that he knew he was the main accused in the dock and said that that was an issue that had to be addressed politically and not through legal processes. He reiterated the stand that Ram temple should be built in Ayodhya, respecting the sentiment of the people, and that this could be done without destroying the mosque. He said that the structure of the mosque would be respectfully relocated and built elsewhere. And he said that even Muslims understood that Ram was a figure of sentiment and respect for the Hindus, and that even Ghalib—he was quoting wrongly because it was Iqbal and not Ghalib—had described Ram as Imam-e-Hind.

At the beginning of his speech, Vajpayee said that he had spoken to Advani the previous night and clarified that Advani did not say that he would participate in the kar seva with a spade and brick. Advani told Vajpayee that those words were put in his mouth by the newspaper report. Vajpayee then proceeded to explain as to why the kar seva was resumed. 'Mr Speaker, Sir, I was not in the country when the decision to resume "Kar Seva" was taken. It needs to be considered deeply as to in what circumstances the decision was taken.'

He cited two reasons. First, he referred to an article of M.G.S. Narayanan, former secretary of Indian Council of Historical Research (ICHR), in the Malayalam newspaper, *Mathrubhumi*, where he alleged that ICHR was deputed to find evidence for the AIBMAC. The other incident Vajpayee referred to was a meeting between Kamal Nath, a minister in Rao's cabinet, who met Advani with a proposal.

> The crux of the proposal was that the Central Government would acquire 2.77 acre of land and hand it over to construct the temple. The decision on disputed structure would be taken through either negotiations or judicial process.... Shri Advaniji remarked that judicial process has been going on for 40 years.... Shri Advaniji had suggested that there should be 'due process of law' in lieu of 'judicial process'. Shri Advaniji had asked him whether this proposal was brought on his own or it had got the support of the Prime Minister also. Shri Kamal Nath replied to Shri Advaniji that it had got the support of the Prime Minister. Later on, we have come to know that he had stated wrongly. That proposal was not supported by the Prime Minister.

Vajpayee argued that the government sent out different messages through different emissaries and this showed 'that there were no definite efforts to solve the problem'.

Then Vajpayee gave credence to the assurance given by the BJP government in Uttar Pradesh:

> Mr. Speaker, Sir, the Government of Uttar Pradesh has given an assurance to the effect that no damage will be allowed to be caused to the disputed structure and it will be totally protected. Therefore, what are the reasons for doubting the assurance of Government of Uttar Pradesh?

Vajpayee's speech was followed by that of Vishwanath Pratap Singh, the former prime minister, then a leader of Janata Dal and a member of parliament (MP) from Fatehpur. Singh showed a rare premonition and confronted the government with the difficult question: if the Uttar Pradesh government refused to deploy the central forces, or if Uttar Pradesh Chief Minister Kalyan Singh were to resign a little before the kar seva on 6 December. Strange questions to ask on 3 December! Singh expostulated like a good politician with a keen awareness of how the local government operates. He said,

> Sir, You have all along been telling us that you would help the State Government. Just now you have said the same thing that whatever force is needed, you will make arrangements for it but you know the right of deployment rests with the State Government. Unless the magistrate issues the order, no action is taken. No doubt, you have every right to send forces anywhere in the country, but everyone knows the fact that unless and until the Magistrate or S.D.M. of a particular area do not order, your force and C.R.P.F do not have any meaning.

Singh very deftly argued that the BJP government, unable to deal with the difficult economic situation in the state, might want to close its shop because its governing was turning out to be unprofitable. Taking a jibe at the BJP's shopkeeper support base, he said,

And if they think that running of Uttar Pradesh Government is an unprofitable venture as the sugarcane growers are resorting to agitations and the labourers are going on strike. On the other side shopkeepers are unhappy as in the name of beautification, they are being displaced and are being [charged] sales tax. Looking at all these things, they might think that this is an unprofitable proposition and since they are business experts, they must close their shop. Then they will not be answerable to fall in the prices of sugarcane, cotton and potatoes, to maintaining law and order and ensuring electricity supply etc. This way they can be free from both and then they may begin to march towards Delhi to launch a campaign on the plea that they will have their own Government in Delhi, they will construct temple. Sir, there may be two ways. They may think [to] close this unprofitable proposition and then Kalyan Singhji may tender his resignation on 5th or 4th saying that my affidavit is no more valid now and I am no more a chief minister....

Apart from Paswan, the man who saw the issue in its fundamental aspect was Syed Shahabuddin, the Janata Dal MP who created the controversy over Salman Rushdie's *The Satanic Verses* in 1988, and who supported the Shah Bano case and threatened to boycott the Republic Day celebrations:

There is no question of confrontation between Hindus and Muslims. But there is a confrontation between the Constitution and those who are prepared to violate it, between the forces of constitutionalism on the one hand and the forces of anti-constitutionalism on the other; between the forces of nationalism and secularism on the one hand, and the forces of chauvinism on the other. Today the secular state is on trial.

Home Minister Chavan, replying to the discussion, adopted a straight-faced stance, which was a clever political pose rather than one of naïvete. He stated in an almost bland language, in response to V.P. Singh's insightful apprehension, which was anything but bland in its implications:

> I am sure that if he (chief minister Kalyan Singh) were to submit his resignation, the BJP will have another person who most probably will be made the Chief Minister (interruptions).... It is as simple as that. So, mere resignation of the chief minister will not solve the problem. The Chief Minister has filed the affidavit on behalf of the Government of U.P. So, he cannot escape the responsibility. When he is saying in categorical terms that they are prepared to give guarantee that orders are not going to be violated and there will be no harm done to the disputed Ram Janambhoomi–Babri Masjid structure, I do not understand why all kinds of doubts are there in their minds.

IX Chapter

APOLOGETICS OF VANDALISM

The kar sevaks stormed the Babri Masjid. It began at around 11:00 AM, and the three domes of the mosque were brought down by around 4:00 PM. The country was stunned into silence. The brinkmanship on the part of BJP just went overboard. The BJP government in Uttar Pradesh headed by Kalyan Singh resigned. The central government dismissed the state government and imposed President's rule. Leader of Opposition in Lok Sabha L.K. Advani resigned from his membership of Parliament, and he was arrested.

When Lok Sabha met on 7 December, there was anger, confusion and disorder. It was like a crowd scene from a Shakespearean play. Vadde Sobhanadreeswara Rao, the TDP member from Vijayawada, said, 'Mr Speaker, this Government have no right to continue. They have failed to protect the structure.' (interruptions) Nirmal Kanti Chatterjee, the CPI(M) member, said, 'The Prime Minister should resign and go.' Digvijay Singh, the Congress member from Rajgarh, was recorded as saying, 'The Prime Minister is going to make a statement.' (interruptions)

No statement could be made, not just on that day but for a whole week. The Lok Sabha was adjourned for a week on 9 December. The speaker pleaded for order, but there was disorder. Members were angry and confused. They did not know how to assess the situation. Speaker Shivraj Patil sounded pathetic when he told the House:

> Listen to me. Such a major incident has occurred. It would not be proper if you don't raise your voice against it in the House. You have to raise the issue. You have to raise your voice against such a major incident. It would not be good if you will not allow to speak. If you want to bring forward

a resolution in the House, you must move it. It would not be good if you don't react. (interruptions)

The disorder continued on 8 December. Atal Bihari Vajpayee requested the speaker to get Advani released so that he could attend the House. Ram Vilas Paswan interjected saying, 'You first ask the Prime Minister to resign and then start the business of the House.' Basudeb Acharia moved an adjournment motion and shouted, 'The entire country is burning and they are the creators of the riot and you are allowing Mr Vajpayee to speak. You should first allow us to speak. More than thousand people have died....' It was adjourned for a week.

A strange development took place when the House met on 17 December. The discussion on the demolition of Babri Masjid came in the form of a no-confidence motion, and it was moved by members of BJP led by Vajpayee. The irony was too stark. BJP, which was responsible for the demolition, should express no confidence in the central government. Vajpayee, in his speech, confessed that the top rank leaders of BJP, RSS and VHP were present, and they tried to prevent the kar sevaks from bringing down the mosque but did not succeed. The incongruity of it simply stares one in the face.

Vajpayee confessed that the commitment made to the prime minister could not be fulfilled. 'We had given an assurance to the Prime Minister. I realise his concern. Arjun Singhji will not realise it. Every effort was made to fufill the commitment given to the Prime Minister. But the commitment could not be fulfilled.' And just before this confession, he even said, 'I would like that an open discussion should take place today. If it concludes that we are at fault then we are ready to accept it.' These were strange words from a member who was moving a no-confidence motion against the government.

He said, 'We have apologised to the journalists who were beaten there. The journalists were beaten and their cameras were broken because the Kar Sevaks did not want their action to be recorded.' And a little before this, he said, 'The top rank leaders of BJP, RSS and VHP had been trying to prevent kar sevaks there. Videotapes are evidence of it.'

Vajpayee tried to put the best spin on the events and hoped that his rhetorical turns would carry the day. He said,

> I am ready to go one step ahead and ask those Kar sevaks who were small in number to come forward and openly confess that they have demolished the structure and for that they are prepared to face the music. I would also like to state there were kar sevaks present in a large number but they were not involved in the demolishing.

Vajpayee's speech resembled that of Brutus after the killing of Julius Caesar in Shakespeare's play of that name. But here was Brutus's speech not with its calm reasoning, but it was infused with emotional pitch of Mark Antony's funeral oration in the play. He pitched it high when he said,

> Ram temple will not be constructed by foul or unfair means. If Ram temple is constructed it would be con-structed on the basis of moral strength. There was no need to assemble large number of karsevaks. Had there been an intention to demolish the structure, it would have been done easily without collecting karsevaks in large number.... So whatever happened there, we regret the incident.

Surprisingly, Vajpayee did not use strong words to express peni-tence or to show that he or his party was ashamed of the act of vandalism. As a matter of fact, the two words, ashamed and van-dalism, did not figure in his speech. And he carefully stuck to the words, regret and incident. He said,

> The press reporters who were there told me that Shri Advani was very sad when the structure was demolished. He was in tears. That is why he has sent in his resignation expressing his regret over the incident. Owning responsi-bility Shri Kalyan Singh also resigned. If you consider it as a drama, then it is a gross misconception because such

type of misconception will neither encourage fair politics in the country nor it will encourage the right secularism.

Vajpayee wove his way in and out from crying 'I am guilty. My party is guilty' to 'The issue was such that nothing could be done. The Hindus were angry and there was no stopping the mob in Ayodhya on that day'. It was a difficult tightrope walk, and he almost stumbled.

He said one moment,

> Mr Speaker, Sir, we had trust in the people. Therefore, we said if the trust of the Hon. Prime Minister has been betrayed, we too are shocked. Shri Kalyan Singh and Shri Advani resigned but nobody from the Central Government is ready to take the blame for it.... Hon. Prime Minister tried his best to stave off any incidents and he tried to resume the 'Kar seva' peacefully and maintain the security of the structure, though it is a fact that he cannot escape from his responsibility.

And from being defensive and apologetic, he went on the offensive: 'But the reaction to the happening in Ayodhya throughout the country and abroad is more or less over-reaction.' He went on to blame the government: 'I think that primarily our outlook and the approach of Government to the problem is no less a factor to be blamed for it.'

Instead of apologising for the destruction of the mosque, Vajpayee faulted the government for not rationalizing the event. He said,

> We did not point out to the world that it was a disputed structure. It was repeatedly stated that there was a mosque. We never clarified that along with the structure of the mosque there is a temple also in which prayer and worship is being done and this dispute has been going on for the last 500 years.

Vajpayee revealed his Hindutva, communalist credentials in a much more aggressive manner than Advani could ever do.

He made two outrageous arguments, defending the demolition of the mosque. First, he referred to a church episode in Poland:

> When Russia occupied Warsaw a church was built there. When Poland became independent, the first thing it did was demolition of the church. History bears testimony to this. When Toynbee visited India he taunted us that it is possible in India alone where a mosque has been created after demolishing the temple.

He was saying, in other words, that demolitions are part of a historical process, and he cited the not very liberal Arnold Toynbee.

Then Vajpayee offered even more outrageous reason for the demolition than the earlier one:

> They do not know that the remnants which have been excavated after demolition now confirm that there was a temple at the site hundreds of years ago. If this fact had been told to the people, then there would have been no uproar to this extent.

He was justifying the demolition because it revealed the truth of the existence of an ancient temple!

This speech of Vajpayee should be remembered in the history of Indian Parliament as the perfect example of sophistry and blatant cynicism. There were moments when Vajpayee's liberal mask slipped, and it is a moot question whether he let it slip consciously or he was not aware of it.

Former Prime Minister Chandra Shekhar in his intervention was quite blunt in his criticism of the government. He asked BJP:

> Shri Advani says that one and a half lakh people were under control and were disciplined and only five hundred people were demolishing the mosque. Were the one and a half lakh so inactive that they could not prevent five hundred persons from demolishing the mosque?

And he told the government:

> The irate mob climbed the mosque at 1.45 pm or 11.30 am on December 6 and the Government remained silent till 6.15 am the next day. Government says that they have been deceived and kept in the dark. You have not been deceived, you have deceived yourself and the people of the country.

There was one sane, sad voice in Lok Sabha in that infamous no-confidence motion debate. It was that of film actor-turned Congress politician from Bombay, Sunil Dutt. He was the only one who could see beyond the demolition of the mosque. He remembered the dead, the people who died in the riots that broke out after the demolition. And without rhetorical flourishes, he damned the rest of the politicians of all parties by his simple, heartfelt and honest intervention.

Speaking on 21 December, Dutt said:

> Today no-confidence motion has been brought against the Government in the House. But in my opinion, here the issue should have been those 1000 persons who have been killed in the aftermath of Ayodhya, about those mothers who lost their sons, about those children who have become orphan and about those women who have become widows. Today no reference is being made about them. Today the discussion is being held as to how will the temple be constructed, how the mosque was demolished. But no reference is being made regarding those over one thousand people who have been killed in the riots. I have deep regret for them.

There could not have been a greater moral rebuke to the political class than this simple statement of Sunil Dutt.

Prime Minister P.V. Narasimha Rao's reply at the end of the debate was intriguing. He took the demolition as a fact and went straight to the point that it should be left behind and that the country should move forward. It was both cynical and pragmatic. Later on, in his speech, he explained the utter helplessness of the central government because it had no other option but to believe the Uttar Pradesh government and all that it could do was to plead until the last to deploy the central forces which were on hand.

Rao seemed to have adopted his soporific tone:

> This country has been a great country. It has risen to great heights, it has seen aberrations but from every aberration it has come out stronger and not weaker. I do hope that this great tragedy, this act of betrayal and vandalism which occurred on the 6th of December will be obliterated as quickly as possible from the public mind. Even the slightest remnant of the memory of this would be harmful to the country and I would appeal to all sections of the people, all sections of the House to help in this process, the process of living down this shameful event of the 6th December and prove to the world once again that this is just an aberration, otherwise the country is full of harmony, full of brotherhood and this has been so for thousands of years, it will be so for thousands of years.

That was a bold, calm way of looking at things after a catastrophic event, asking the people to forget and move on. Rao maintained his poise. He did not become outright self-righteous. He did not give in to despair. He explained the reasons for trusting BJP, but he did not blame BJP too much or for too long.

Later in his rather concise reply, Rao expanded on the issue of trust between the central government and the state government, between the state government and the Supreme Court. He expostulated:

> It is rather strange, Mr Speaker, Sir, that this discussion should come in the form of a No-Confidence Motion. The Bharatiya Janata Party has no confidence in the Government of India. Why? Because the Government of India reposed confidence in the State Government of the Bharatiya Janata Party. May be, this is good justice meted

out to the Government of India. I have to own that. But how do we run the country? How do Centre–State relations run? On the basis of suspicion? On the basis of mistrust?

And he let out his own hunch:

> But is it possible, is it conceivable for the Central Government of any federation to even imagine that one of the units, a State Government, would keep giving affidavit after affidavit after affidavit, giving solemn assurances, and finally violate those assurances in a manner that until the last moment cannot be detected? That is why my first reaction was that for all appearances it was pre-planned. There is going to be an enquiry. I would not like to anticipate their results or the findings of the enquiry. But it was so planned, it cannot be an accident, it just cannot be an accident.

Vajpayee and Rao used their speech skills in different ways. Starting on an apologetic note, Vajpayee ended on an aggressive one. Vajpayee, though moving the no-confidence motion against the government, did not make the case that the Rao government should quit. His speech was more in defence of BJP and what it did and did not do in Ayodhya on 6 December 1992. The BJP leader was more than sympathetic to the prime minister. The government did no wrong except for not urging the courts to deliver the judgment in the Ayodhya case. But that was not really the fault of the government. Rao tried to remain detached and calm, and even when he blamed BJP, he did so in terms of systemic functioning. He did not accuse BJP of communalism. Nor did he say that a party like BJP had no place in the secular polity of India. He was aware that BJP was winning seats and votes and steadily increasing its strength in the House. He had to speak in terms of the Centre–state relations and not in terms of the opposed ideologies of Congress and BJP. The other members of Congress such as Digvijay Singh and Mani Shankar Aiyar did that. Rao kept away from that line of argument.

The no-confidence motion was defeated overwhelmingly with 334 noes as against 106 ayes.

On 23 December, Lok Sabha discussed the Dunkel Draft with regard to the setting up of the World Trade Organization (WTO), the successor to the General Agreement on Tariffs and Trade (GATT). Ayodhya was pushed into the background as a 'bad memory' as much as possible, something that Rao wanted. But the people did not forget it at election time in 1996.

Dramatis Personae

P.V. Narasimha Rao, the Reluctant Reformer

In 1991, the party had accepted Narasimha Rao only as a replacement, with the knowledge and awareness that it rightfully belonged to Sonia Gandhi. For many observers, analysts and critics, including members of Opposition parties, it is this attachment of the party for the family that is the bane of Congress. The party had always brushed aside the criticism and objection with unconcealed contempt and perverse glee. In 1991, no one knew how long Narasimha Rao would survive. He survived the term from 1991 to 1996. It was the first time after Lal Bahadur Shastri, who was the prime minister between June 1964 and January 1966, that there was a Congress prime minister who was not a Nehru–Gandhi. Narasimha Rao did not cover himself with glory. He was derided both by his party and by the Opposition. Those who praised his wiliness and cunning really wanted to get the better of him as soon as they could. When Congress lost the 1996 election, it was just a matter of time before he was dethroned as the leader of CPP and as party president. Narasimha Rao did not put up any fight as he was unceremoniously thrown out. The few friends he had kept away and the detractors saw to it that Congress made no mention of him in any way. In 2003 AICC session in New Delhi, Narasimha Rao was invited and he sat on the dais quietly next to Party President Sonia Gandhi. She was courteous towards him.

Narasimha Rao did not make any statements that would embarrass the party. He wrote his stuff, spent time at the computer and attended book launches. One of them was at Taj Mansingh hotel in New Delhi where Navtej Sarna's, who was the foreign office spokesperson, novel *We Weren't Lovers Like That* was launched. The other was at 7, Race Course Road, the prime minister's residence, where he was present for the release of the autobiographical volumes of D.P. Mishra, a key Indira Gandhi supporter who was estranged from her later by his son Brajesh Mishra, national security adviser to Prime Minister Atal Bihari Vajpayee. Narasimha Rao spoke fondly of the elder Mishra. The rest of the time, Narasimha Rao kept to himself. He gave an interview to Shekhar Gupta of the *Indian Express* but said that he would not divulge as to what really happened with regard to United States' pressure on India from conducting the Agni, the missile capable of carrying a nuclear bomb, test. He said that it would go with him to his grave. He also said that he stood like a rock behind his Finance Minister Manmohan Singh to pursue the economic reforms programme.

In a surprise move, he wrote a three-part article in the *Indian Express*, arguing against the privatization of the national carriers, Air India and Indian Airlines, and that reform of public sector did not mean selling them off. In a riposte, P. Chidambaram commented that he thought that there were three reformers—he, Manmohan Singh and Narasimha Rao—and now he would have to say there were just two and a half reformers, mocking Narasimha Rao for not being fully there on the side of reform.

Rao was never a vocal market economy advocate. He felt that he was bringing about the changes within the Congress framework of socialism and that it was not a break with socialism. He did not become the follower of either Friedrich Hayek, the Austrian economist who was vehemently opposed to state intervention in times of economic crisis, a remedy championed by doctrinal rival John Maynard Keynes, or the unleashing of unbridled market forces as advocated by right-wing American economist Milton Friedman. Rao ploughed his furrow of economic reforms within the narrow confines of Congress socialism. He was a socialist conservative compared to Rajiv Gandhi who chafed at the socialist shackles and who wanted to break free. Rao was the party man who was at home with the tried-and-tested ideology of socialism and populism that Indira Gandhi had perfected, and who was pushing through the market reforms of the economy quietly, if not surreptitiously, through the crevices of state-managed socialism.

On 17 August 1996, Narasimha Rao wrote a terse, stoic letter to an ailing P. Sadasiva, a brilliant polymath and friend of his younger days in Warangal:

> My dear Sadasiv, I am in receipt of your letter written by Niranjan. This is the time for courage and fortitude. I am sure you and the family members are bearing with the difficult time. I hope things will improve, as in many cases it has happened. I am also passing through an extremely trying period. There are too many complications and absolutely unfounded acts of political vendetta directed both against myself and the party. I have a mind to pay a visit to Warangal to see you. But right now I am not able to move. Let us see. God help us all. Be cheerful and confident. Yours affly,
> P.V. Narasimha Rao.

Sadasiva died on 26 August. (The letter is available on the Internet at kakatiyapatrika.com and it had been put up by Sadasiva's family in 2011.)

It was a sad letter of a man who had no one to share his sadness with. His loneliness was complete in the days after he laid down office. He stayed alone at his residence at 9, Motilal Nehru Marg, New Delhi. Very few people visited him. He kept to himself, and he kept his thoughts to himself. The letter to his friend gives a rare glimpse of what he felt towards a dying friend. The stoicism he counselled to Sadasiva was perhaps something that he was himself practising.

He was sceptical of reforms and revolutions. He was a conservative and even a bit of a reactionary in his personal/private beliefs. But like many educated Indians, his was a many-layered intellectual life, with rationality and high-minded, which could sound hollow at times, spiritualism at one end, and undeclared piety and superstition at the other. He kept the contradictions in place, leaving many who wanted to get him right quite bewildered.

He spoke with detachment about the reforms he had allowed Manmohan Singh to unleash in the Samuel L. and Elizabeth Jodidi Memorial Lecture at Harvard University on 17 May 1994. Rajiv Gandhi delivered the same memorial lecture in 1987. Rao's lecture was reproduced in *Mainstream* weekly in the 16 July 2011 edition, and it revealed a man far removed from what he was doing. He showed no passion for reforms as these two short passages from the lecture show:

> Jawaharlal Nehru named India's economic system as mixed economy; not a mechanical part-admixture of the other two systems, but a complete system by itself, in which some features of those who happened to find place. True to the liberal tradition—of which your great institution is a custodian—India has never looked at progress as a single, unidirectional straight and narrow path. It has always been cyclical in its outlook. For every assertion there is a negation, for every postulate a counter-postulate. There can never be only One. If there is Zero, shunya, there is also Infinity, poorna. In between, if there is One there must be Another. Therefore, one society cannot completely be replicated in another, each has to fashion its own way for itself.

> However, one fact has become abundantly clear, that the roles of the State and the market are essentially distinct and complete usurpation of the role of the one by the other is neither possible nor desirable. While assigning the role to each at a given time, the current situation in the society has necessarily to be taken into account. And neither will wither away, no matter what one hypnotises oneself to believe in a given context. But the transition to the post-Cold War World, welcome as it is, is likely to be even more difficult than ending the Cold War. The days of rejoicing at the demise of the old system are over.

> The contours of a different world have begun to emerge, a world so different from the world of blocs and deterrences that we have almost forgotten.

He was literally beating about the bush, not accepting the need for economic reforms in the country. And he struggled to explain or assert what was India's view in a post-Cold War world. India could not decide, and this lack of clarity was reflected in his opinion about the situation at the end of the Cold War. Despite his interest in intellectual things, Rao did not muster the courage and clarity to state India's view and position. Rao's intellectual unpreparedness was also that of the country's intelligentsia. Rao could not fall back on a national debate which could give him the reference points for stating the Indian view.

Given Rao's mix of political socialism and social conservatism, it might appear that he pursued the policy of reforms almost in a fit of absent-mindedness in the manner of those at the helm of East India Company who had acquired an Indian empire before they realized what they had done, and then tried to find reasons for justifying it. It is more likely that Rao let reforms happen, though he did not believe in them because he recognized that they were necessary. Most of Rao's simple-minded left-liberal critics took his social conservatism to be Hindu communalism. There were reasons enough to suspect him of being crypto-RSS ideologue, but he meticulously maintained the politically correct Congress stance of secularism.

Rao's politics resemble that of US presidents Lyndon Johnson and of Richard Nixon. Johnson was the Democratic successor to the charismatic John F. Kennedy in the White House in the turbulent 1960s. It was Johnson, the hard-headed Texan politician, who got the Civil Rights Bill passed, which was a huge step in meeting the aspirations of the Blacks in the country, and he ushered in the concept of Great Society, which expanded the welfare sphere of the government. Nixon, an ardent Republican Cold warrior and the only president to be impeached in the history of the United States, was not an inspiring figure. But he did many things right. He reached out to China of Mao after 20 years of blinkered US policy of not recognizing the government that ruled over the most populous country in the world. The ping-pong diplomacy that culminated in Nixon's visit to Beijing and his meeting with Mao Zedong came in the middle of the theatre of cruelty, the Cultural Revolution, which began in and around 1966 and ended around 1976. Nixon was in Beijing in 1972. The United States needed, or felt it needed, Pakistan to connect with China. It was one of the reasons that Nixon and his man Friday, Henry Kissinger, were hostile to India during the Bangladesh War. And he pulled the US troops out of the Vietnam War. Johnson was no F.D. Roosevelt, but he did what he did because he knew it needed to be done. Nixon was as tough an anti-communist as any American Cold warrior was, but he saw the strategic imperative of connecting with China. A good politician does the right thing, whether he believes in it or not. He does it because he knows that it needs to be done. So it was with Johnson, with Nixon and with Rao.

BJP'S MOMENT OF TRUTH

There was an imbalance in the political spectrum. The right end of the spectrum was vacant for a long time. Congress, the socialists and the communists occupied the left end of the spectrum, each competing with the other as to who would profess socialist economy more convincingly and who among them would implement it more effectively. The socialists were nowhere near power until 1967. It was only in that election in Uttar Pradesh and Bihar that the socialists found themselves in seats of power in these two states. In Uttar Pradesh, it was a coalition government led by Samyukta Vidhayak Dal (SVD) led by Charan Singh, a former Congressman. He was not a socialist, but he championed the cause of the farmers and showed an aversion to industry and technology. In Bihar, the government of Karpoori Thakur was socialist enough, but it was led by the intermediate castes. The communists had a short stint in power in Kerala in 1957, but the first democratically elected communist government was brought down by Congress in the state which was dominated by the landed interests of the Christians in the state. The communists posed a direct challenge to the church and its economically influential parishioners which had a stranglehold on land and educational institutions. The communists had to wait until 1977, for 20 years, to form government in West Bengal.

The right-wing BJS was formed in 1951 by Syama Prasad Mookerjee, who was until then the leader of the Hindu Mahasabha. The Jana Sangh could not make any impact. In the crisis moment of 1977 when many of the Opposition parties were occupying the central segment of the political spectrum, the rump Congress that Indira Gandhi left behind when she broke away in 1969, the Swatantra Party and the Jana Sangh formed the Janata Party. Swatantra Party was a truly right-wing party, which had opposed tooth and nail the state domination and state management of the economy. The party founded by another former Congressman C. Rajagopalachari, the first Indian governor-general of Independent India, favoured private enterprise, and in the then prevailing Cold War between the capitalist and democratic West and the communist-socialists in the Soviet Union and eastern European countries, the party wanted that India should be in the democratic and capitalist Western camp. Congress and Nehru favoured socialism and, though maintaining neutrality between the two Cold War camps, were more sympathetic to the communist countries because Soviet Union and its satellites were firmly on the side of the former colonies of Western countries in Asia and Africa. Nehru's Congress, and later Indira Gandhi's Congress, could not resist the anti-imperialist and anti-colonial rhetoric of the communist bloc. The Jana Sangh was staunchly anti-communist, but it did not articulate clearly the philosophy of free enterprise and free market. Swatantra Party formed governments in Orissa, Rajasthan, Gujarat and Madhya Pradesh in 1967. These non-Congress governments were defeated in the heightened socialist rhetoric and populism of Indira Gandhi in the 1971 election.

The Jana Sangh, which emerged with the Janata Party, re-emerged as BJP in 1980 after 100 MPs of the earlier Jana Sangh walked out when the socialist wing of the Janata Party led by Madhu Limaye objected to the affiliation of the former Jana Sangh members to the Hindu right-wing organization, RSS, what came to be known as the dual-membership issue. BJP remained in the shadows in the 1980s because of the catastrophic assassination of Indira Gandhi in 1984. It came into its own only in 1989, when it won 80 seats in the Lok Sabha.

The rise of BJP between 1989 and 1998 was quite impressive, even spectacular. The right-wing party had at last come into its own, and this time it had no rival at the right end because the Swatantra Party was not there. BJP was not just a right-wing party but also a Hindu right-wing party, and it was willing to be seen as the party of the majority Hindus. It adopted a stance which all communal parties adopt. It said that it did not want majority Hindus to be at a disadvantage in the name of secularism and the defence of the rights and liberties of religious minorities. Muslim parties such as IUML and the Hyderabad-based Majlis-e-Ittehadul Muslimeen (MIM) had always argued that they were defending the interests of the minority Muslim community and this should not be seen as being anti-Hindu. It was the same argument that SAD, the political offshoot of the Shiromani Gurdwara Prabandhak Committee (SGPC), had also argued. BJP also argued that it was pro-Hindu and that it was not anti-Muslim or anti-Christian or anti-Sikh. In practice, none of these parties could convince people who belonged to other communities. BJP was perceived as anti-Muslim and anti-Christian; the Muslim parties did not inspire confidence among the majority Hindus. Sikh terrorists in Punjab in the early 1980s, preceding Operation Blue Star of June 1984, targeted the majority Hindus, especially the followers of RSS. The Akali Dal became the communal face and voice of the Sikhs. The alliances that emerged among the respective communal parties are interesting. BJP and the Akali Dal came together post 1996, and Muslim parties such as MIM and IUML became part of the United Progressive Alliance (UPA) led by Congress in 2004.

BJP's electoral fortunes improved incrementally from the 1989 election onwards. The electoral graph of BJP between 1989 and 2009 shows an interesting rise and fall of the party. The numbers tell the story better than anything else. In the 1989 election, BJP won 85 seats out of the 225 it had contested, and its vote share stood at 11.36 per cent. In the 1991 election, the party won 120 seats, but it had contested 468 seats. Its percentage share of votes stood at 20.11 per cent. In 1996, BJP got 161 seats out of the 471 it had contested, and its share of votes improved marginally to 20.29 per cent. Congress, in contrast, had 140 seats out of the 529 it had contested, and its share of votes stood at a much higher 28.80 per cent compared to that of BJP. In 1998, BJP hit the peak with 182 seats and its share of votes rose to 25.59 per cent. BJP could not cross this barrier. In the 1999 elections, it retained its 182 seats, but the share of votes declined to 23.75 per cent. Interestingly, in 1998, Congress had 141 seats and its share of votes stood at 25.82 per cent, marginally higher than that of BJP.

And in 1999, Congress was reduced to 114 seats, but its share of votes stood at a high of 28.30 per cent.

The communists and other parties of socialist centre and regional parties such as TDP and Janata Dal were in no mood to accept the fact that BJP had forged ahead in 1996. CPI(M)'s Sitaram Yechury argued that the vote was in favour of the secular parties. And he seemed to be right going by the share of votes of the Congress party and the others. But parliamentary democracy was about numbers. President Shankar Dayal Sharma asked Atal Bihari Vajpayee to form the government and prove his majority on the floor of the Lok Sabha. In the trust motion debate that followed in the Lok Sabha, it became evident that BJP stood isolated and that the other non-Congress parties were unwilling to support it. It was a bitter lesson for Vajpayee and for BJP. When he saw the arguments going against his party in debate, Vajpayee walked out of Lok Sabha without waiting for the vote to be taken and submitted his resignation to the president. Defeat was staring BJP in the face. The first BJP government lasted for 13 days.

This short stint was also the moment of truth for BJP. It learnt that it did not have the numbers of its own and that the other parties that summer of 1996 would not allow it to pass through the portals of power successfully. The vote of confidence that Atal Bihari Vajpayee moved on 27 May was a tipping point in Indian politics in many ways. It was the first time that a party associated with Hindu majoritarianism came as near as it could to the seat of power and found that it will not be able to go beyond that point.

Vajpayee moving the motion of confidence was aware that BJP did not stand much of a chance, but he used the occasion cleverly to soften the image of the party post demolition of Babri Masjid in Ayodhya three and a half years earlier. The common perception is that BJP made the gains it made because of the Ayodhya agitation and that it has managed to win the support of a significant chunk of Hindu votes. This will remain a debating point that whether the Hindu majority had turned communal and it was ready to accept the political credo of a party that spoke up for

Hindus as such. The only state where it seemed to reflect this mood was through it predominance in the state of Uttar Pradesh where it had won 50 of the 85 seats.

It was left to Vajpayee to make the best case for BJP in the same way he tried to do for the party after the demolition. In the no-confidence motion that BJP moved against the Narasimha Rao government, Vajpayee had to do the impossible thing of accepting the fact of demolition and deflecting the blame from the party. He barely managed to do it. But in May 1996, he had a relatively easy task of presenting a positive side of his party.

Vajpayee had to face up to the charge of communalism and he did:

> The biggest allegation levelled against us is that we are a communal party and we lack secular credentials and as such let all the guardians of the so-called secularism unite and vote the BJP out of power. Democracy is a game of numbers which is not in our favour. We have got the largest popular mandate.

He was aware that the United Front (UF) was only too ready to step in and he accepted the possibility with caveats: 'If United Front comes forward with a programme and assures us that because of political ambition and obsession for power no bitter experiences of the past will be allowed to repeat, only then people may feel a bit assured.' He also pointed out with reference to Ayodhya: 'The Ayodhya incident took place much later but we were being branded as communalists and non-secular much before it.'

Then he talked about infiltration from Bangladesh into Assam:

> If someone comes for a job and returns after completing it, then it is a separate thing. The arrangement of work permit can be made for such people but the report of the Home Ministry says that the infiltrators come in lakhs through the rivers and by hiding in the bushes.

Biju Patnaik, a senior leader from Orissa, intervened:

> Mr. Prime Minister, you started so well on your line of persuasion. Many of us thought that we will go and join you, but in the mean time you touched on points that dissuaded us from joining. Do you realise what you have done and why you have done it? When you talk of secularism and non-secularism you are propagating the vice of non-secularism, and why? That was not your intention. Why have you done it?

Vajpayee answered:

> Mr. Speaker, Sir, a very senior Member of this House and an old colleague of mine Shri Biju Patnaik has raised very important issue here. I would like to say that on the issue of secularism we must talk with an open mind and with some seriousness. (interruptions) The Bharatiya Janata Party has made it clear on more than one occasion that they are committed to the Constitution, to the secularism as enshrined in the Constitution.... (interruptions) The state should be secular. India has always been a secular state. There will be no danger to the secular structure of the country in future.

He explained that India was not born in 1947, that it was a 5,000-year old civilization, and that during the discussion on secularism in the Constituent Assembly, different views were expressed and 'the framers of the Constitution did not incorporate the word secular in the Constitution.' He also said that the word 'secular' was incorporated in the Preamble of the Constitution during the Emergency, 'when several leaders were in jails and there was no freedom of expression'. But Vajpayee had no objection to the amendment brought to insert 'secular' in the Preamble, though he noted, 'Earlier, the opinion was that the Preamble of the Constitution should and shall not be amended....' He said that he had gone through the debate on the amendment—the infamous 42nd Amendment to the Constitution—and noted:

> At that time every member belonging to the Congress Party especially Sardar Swaran Singh had emphasised that their secularism would be quite different from that of the Western countries. He said that since India is a multi-religious country and secularism means that there should not be any discrimination against the followers of different religions and all religions should be equally treated.

And he concurred in the argument: 'We wholeheartedly accept this interpretation of religion.' And he added: 'This is the quintessence of Hindu ideology.' He went on to assure: 'We will never make our country a theocratic state like our neighbouring countries.' But he could not restrain himself from asking: 'But does it mean that we do not have our own roots and civilisation? Does it mean that we have no values of life?' Clearly, Vajpayee and those who had thought over the issue of secularism thought that secularism was not amenable to roots and values and to civilization. It was an interesting ambiguity, and it was beyond the intellectual realm and ability of Vajpayee and his party to think through it. Vajpayee the politician understood the pressing issue of the politics of the hour.

He was also aware that questions were being raised as to why the president had asked BJP to form the government and seek vote of confidence when it was clear that the party did not have the necessary support. He said at the very beginning of his speech:

> This controversy has been going for so many days as to why the President has invited me to form the Government. It has disturbed the sleep of many people.... Some people have uttered such words for the President which should not have been used. But what else the President could do in the post-election scenario? Whether he should have called the Congress which was defeated in the elections and lost the mandate and whose rule the people rejected? Whether he should have called a weird assortment of heterogenous elements which had not come into existence till then? If the hon. President has invited the BJP

as the largest single party, he has acted according to constitutional propriety and the democratic norms.

Vajpayee's sophistry failed to win over the sceptics in other parties or blunt the criticism of the opponents. Chandra Shekhar, who was prime minister for four months after the V.P. Singh government fell in 1990, a seasoned politician who saw through the masks of ideology on all sides of the political stage, made the simple point: 'I am not one of those people who want that the BJP in any case should not form the Government. In the democracy, if the BJP gets majority, they will form the Government.' It was a clear hint to Vajpayee and BJP that they did not have the majority. He also pointed out that apart from the Samata Party, Akali Dal and Shiv Sena, other political parties did not offer to support BJP. Chandra Shekhar also said that he did not form his government until Rajiv Gandhi's letter went to the president declaring support for his government. It was again a rebuff to Vajpayee that he had no ground to stand on.

Sharad Pawar, a political pragmatist like Chandra Shekhar, was more forthright:

> Those who always talk of majority are enjoying power today in spite of having no hope for absolute majority in the House.... It will be written in the history of our country that by staking false claim of getting absolute majority, BJP has blemished the democratic tradition of the country for getting power only for a few days.

He also reminded Vajpayee of the fascist mood of the right-wing grouping: 'And in Mumbai, Shri Bal Thackeray said that if the BJP government falls then there will be a civil war in the country. It proves that you have no faith in democracy.'

Somnath Chatterjee of CPI(M) was more unsparing in his criticism of the 11-day BJP government, 'They came to be sworn in on 16th and today is 27th', and he pointed out the impropriety of the Vajpayee cabinet approving the 'counter-guarantees of the Enron Power Project' in a special meeting on 27 May. He flayed the government in stinging language:

> You are on the threshold of losing your position today. In the absence of any claim of any majority even now ... such an important decision is being taken on the day this confidence motion is being discussed. The cabinet of this country which is on trial, yet to prove its mandate is taking a very important decision of approving this counter-guarantee.

And an angry Chatterjee continued:

> For five hours now we are discussing this motion and not for once, neither the Prime Minister nor his present supporter Mr Fernandes has claimed this that this government has the majority support of the House. Then, what is this exercise going on! That is why we had made a request to put this motion to vote without any discussion. We felt that this Constitutional aberration called Vajpayee government should be ended immediately without any ritual.

There was then fierce opposition from all sides to BJP forming a government. The opposition came from the communist and the socialist parties. Congress opposed, but it had lost the election. It was not just that BJP did not have numbers of its own—and this is something it could not achieve in 1998 and in 1999 as well—but also that it could not convince other parties to join a broader coalition in 1996. It became clear that a purely right-wing formation can never form a government in India, though it had happened by then in Maharashtra where the Shiv Sena and BJP were running a coalition government and it had happened in Gujarat where BJP was running a government on its own strength.

It was the turn of UF formation to form the government. Karnataka Chief Minister H.D. Deve Gowda was chosen to be the prime minister after much feverish speculation. The confidence motion was taken up on 12 June, a fortnight after the failed attempt of BJP. P.V. Narasimha Rao made a surprise intervention. He did not speak in the motion of confidence moved by Vajpayee. Rao made it clear that Congress would support the UF government because

Rajiv Gandhi to Narendra Modi

it could not support a BJP government. And he set out the ideological incompatibility between Congress and BJP, which made it impossible for Congress to support BJP. He did not build his argument on the simple antithesis between secularism represented by Congress and communalism represented by BJP. He said that it was Indira Gandhi who inserted the word 'secular' in the Preamble of the Constitution but the Constitution and the polity were secular even before that. He argued in quite a cynical and perverse manner that there could not ever be a common civil code, one of the issues that BJP insisted on but it did not want to insist on the contentious issue along with the other two: Article 370, which granted a special status to Jammu and Kashmir, and the building of the Ram temple on the site of the demolished Babri Masjid at Ayodhya. Rao argued that Hindus could not accept a common civil code because of their peculiar marriage customs. For instance, a girl is allowed to marry her mother's brother in South India and this was frowned upon in North India. So there could not be a common civil code for Hindus because of the regional variation in marriage customs. Then he extended the argument to Muslims who were allowed to marry cousins on their paternal side. Like Vajpayee, Rao was indulging in casuistry. Pawar's opposition to Congress was simple and straightforward.

The UF interlude turned out to be brief, though it did offer some hope that there could be a non-Congress, non-BJP government at the Centre. The weakness of the UF government was that it depended on Congress for its survival. An angry home minister and CPI leader Indrajit Gupta told the Congress members in the Lok Sabha in the course of a debate that people would throw shoes at them if they were to rock the government. It did not prevent Congress from forcing UF to replace Deve Gowda as prime minister. The job then went to Inder Kumar Gujral. Deve Gowda was a feisty Karnataka politician who fought for his place in the state when the charismatic Ramakrishna Hegde gained an upper hand and enjoyed popular support. But it was beyond Gowda's political skills to humour Congress, which was necessary for his survival, and no one missed him when he stepped down. Gujral with his sophisticated profile could not hold as well.

He fell when it was revealed that the Jain Commission looking into the assassination of Rajiv Gandhi had blamed the role of Dravida Munnetra Kazhagam (DMK), and Congress demanded that the DMK ministers be removed from the cabinet. The UF government had to go.

When Vajpayee came back to stake the BJP's claim to form a government on 27 March 1998, he abandoned his eloquence and turned pragmatic. He did not claim civilizational virtues for BJP, and he harped on the theme of continuity. Vajpayee recalled his stint as foreign minister in the Morarji Desai government of the Janata Party in 1977 and narrated an incident to emphasize his theme of continuity: 'At that time a foreign diplomat had asked me as a Foreign Minister as to what change was going to take place in the South block where I sat. Thereupon I replied that nothing was going to change, only the Minister has changed.'

He also recalled that he had got replaced a picture of Nehru which used to hang in the ministry and which went missing when he took over as minister in 1977. Vajpayee was seeking reconciliation, and he turned a raconteur to drive home his point:

> Once I told Panditji that he was a man of mixed personality that he was Churchill, as well as Chamberlain also. He did not mind it. On the same day we met at a banquet. He told (sic) that my speech was very powerful, then he smiled and went away. Today, such a criticism would invite animosity and the people would stop speaking.

Then he posed the rhetorical question: 'Can't we, the leaders of the country co-operate with each other and face the challenges before the nation unitedly?'

Sharad Pawar was steadfast in his criticism of BJP. He pointed out the contradictions in the BJP's stand on swadeshi in the context of economic reforms. He said that when Gandhi used swadeshi to galvanize the nationalist sentiment against the colonial ruler, it was a different time. He pointed out that the foreign direct investment in the country was 2 per cent of the GDP, and that it could not pose a threat. While recalling the BJP's opposition to the Enron project while in opposition, he was happy that the 13-day BJP government in May 1996 cleared the project.

Congress had to play dirty with UF because of its own political compulsions. It seemed that if Congress allowed UF a smooth ride, then Congress might lose its electoral legitimacy. It was much more in the interests of Congress that BJP should be in power because that would create polarization between the two parties. UF was a poor cousin of Congress and the poor cousin should not be allowed to stay in the arc lights for too long. Congress perceived Deve Gowda to be chasing some of the Congress leaders like its president Kesri for corruption. In the case of Gujral, a former Congressman, the findings of the Jain Commission into the assassination of Rajiv Gandhi revealed the support that DMK, one of the partners in the ruling UF, gave to LTTE. Congress wanted Gujral to drop the DMK ministers. And the Gujral government was toppled. It was this action that forced DMK into the arms of BJP and its alliance of National Democratic Alliance (NDA) in 1999. In 1998, Congress toppled the Vajpayee government with the margin of a single vote but failed to form a government of its own. This led to the 1999 election, which BJP won rather comfortably with its NDA partners. It was after this that Congress learned the art of patience and of sitting in the opposition for the five-year term, and it did not create any instability. Supporters of Congress were unhappy that the party was not taking to the streets the way Indira Gandhi did after she lost the 1977 election. They blamed and made fun of Sonia Gandhi's lack of initiative and her political inexperience. Sonia Gandhi learnt her bitter lesson when she trusted Subramanian Swamy, J. Jayalalithaa and Mulayam Singh Yadav. When UPA was formed in 2003–2004, All India Anna Dravida Munnetra Kazhagam (AIADMK), Subramanian Swamy and Mulayam Singh Yadav did not have a place in it. Congress had not closed the door on Mulayam Singh Yadav. When the Left Front withdrew support in 2008, Mulayam Singh Yadav lent his support to the UPA government. This did not lead to the cementing of an alliance between UPA and Mulayam Singh Yadav's Samajwadi Party (SP) in 2009 Lok Sabha elections, but they remained in touch with each other. Mulayam Singh Yadav had lost the 2007 assembly election to Mayawati in Uttar Pradesh, and it made sense for him to cosy up to Congress at the Centre. It was clear to Congress and to Mulayam Singh Yadav that they could not be allies because Congress was not willing to abandon its space in Uttar Pradesh. In 2009, Congress won 21 Lok Sabha seats from Uttar Pradesh. Congress and SP remained uneasy partners with SP having won the 2012 assembly election in the state and Congress still holding the reins of power at the Centre.

XI Chapter

ROMANCING PAKISTAN

The Vajpayee government's six years in office were marked by interesting and important turns and twists, especially with regard to Pakistan. It will be difficult to analyse the place of Pakistan in BJP's political imagination. There is, however, no doubt that Pakistan was one of the main reference points for BJP to make its political mark. This was never openly stated. The political Hindu right wing looked to an undivided India where the Hindus, the majority of the population, had the pride of place. The Muslim separatists saw the ploy and argued for special protection for Muslims in the early years, and in the late 1930s and in the 1940s for a separate Muslim state. The Muslim leaders saw Congress as a Hindu organization and they did not pay any attention to the Hindu right-wingers themselves. The Hindu right wing felt slighted by the fact that the separatist Muslim leadership did not pay any attention to it and directed their ire against Congress. The Jana Sangh and later BJP had always positioned themselves as tough in the case of Pakistan and tried to portray Congress as weak-kneed when it came to dealing with Pakistan. The truth was that Congress was tough with Pakistan and soft with Muslims in India. BJP tried to interpret Congress's soft approach towards Muslims in India as being soft towards Pakistan. The leaders in Pakistan were well aware that Congress was the tough cookie, and they hated Congress for it. When BJP came to power for the first time, one of the ways it had to define its political space depended on how it dealt with Pakistan.

After winning the confidence motion at the end of March 1998, NDA announced the successful testing of nuclear weapons capability in May 1998. BJP was trying to make a political statement that it wanted to project India as a muscular state. The last time India tested its nuclear capability was in 1974, at a time when

Indira Gandhi was facing political discontent all over the country. It is not clear as to why Indira Gandhi decided that there should be a nuclear test. India was capable of carrying out one in the 1960s as well, and there was pressure from the hawks that India should carry out the test to declare its military capability. The tests were not necessary to harness nuclear technology for generating electricity. India was already doing it on a small scale with the help of technological assistance from Canada and the United States under the Atoms for Peace programme. After the 1962 military debacle with China, the hawks looked to the nuclear bomb as a way of defending India. China had moved far ahead in terms of nuclear explosions and weapons capability. China had carried out the hydrogen bomb explosion in 1964 at a time when India was arguing for nuclear disarmament, especially at the Non-Aligned meet at Congress. It is true that after the 1971 military defeat, a humiliated Pakistan under Zulfiqar Ali Bhutto was keen to acquire the bomb, and the intemperate and nearly insane Bhutto talked of the Pakistan bomb as the Islamic bomb. Bhutto wanted to show Pakistan to be the defender of the Muslim countries and hence the first convention of the Organisation of Islamic Countries (OIC) held in Islamabad. The Indian dilemma in 1974 could be seen as genuine, to explode or not to explode the bomb. The 1974 test was not of weapons grade. Critics, however, point out that this was a veneer and that the real motive behind the test was military. In 1998, the internal and external compulsions seemed to be of a different kind. It was clear in the 1990s that Pakistan had a clandestine nuclear weapons programme. The second Indian test provoked Pakistan to carry out its own version of the nuclear tests, eight of which compared to India's five in the second half of May 1998. Pakistani Prime Minister Nawaz Sharif adopted an extremely moderate tone and refuted the idea of the Islamic bomb, which was the fantasy of Bhutto, and made it clear that it was geared to boost Pakistan's own military defence. That had sobered the Indian elation, especially in the BJP ranks immediately after the tests of 11 May. One of BJP's leaders from Delhi, Madan Lal Khurana, thumped his thighs—a traditional Indian wrestler's way of challenging his opponent in the mud pit—and thundered that India would take on anyone who dared to challenge it.

In February 1999, Vajpayee travelled to Lahore in a bus, accompanied by a galaxy of Indian celebrities as a goodwill gesture. He visited Minar-e-Pakistan, and it was seen in Pakistan as a significant gesture from the right-wing Hindus, as an acknowledgement of the existence of Pakistan and as an abandonment of Undivided India or Akhand Bharat.

This was, however, followed by the Kargil episode in May–June 1999 when infiltrators from Pakistan occupied the hilltops along the road from Srinagar to Leh. The Indian Army had a tough time regaining the hilltops. Four hundred Indian soldiers died. There was pressure from the United States to end the conflagration. The remaining intruders were allowed to get back to Pakistan. The government claimed that it managed to regain the lost heights and termed it a victory. NDA wanted to celebrate it as Vijay Diwas. The Army reminded that Vijay Diwas was already being celebrated on 16 December, the day Dhaka fell to the Indian forces in 1971 and there should not be confusion.

Kargil remained a problematic episode for BJP and NDA. BJP wanted to turn it into a victory parade, but it was not a decisive military victory as in 1965 and in 1971. Kargil had echoes of the 1962 war with China. As in 1962 so in 1999, the Army and the government were taken by surprise. In 1999, US President Bill Clinton pressurized Pakistani Prime Minister Nawaz Sharif to back off. And India yielded ground too by giving a 'safe passage' to the infiltrators-cum-jihadis to get out of the Indian territory. This was seen as a victory by BJP. The Subrahmanyam Committee was set up to look at the weaknesses in the intelligence system in the Armed Forces and elsewhere. One of the conclusions that the committee arrived at was that there was a communication gap between the military intelligence and the Intelligence Bureau. Kargil was an episode in the six-year-old NDA tenure and not the great military engagement that BJP could rest on its laurels. Even Indira Gandhi could not rest on the laurels of the military victory in Bangladesh in 1971, though she played a decisive role in it. BJP was taken by surprise at Kargil. An emotional former Indian cricket team captain Kapil Dev said that there should be no cricket matches with Pakistan and the government agreed. The stand-off did not last. Vajpayee made another attempt to strike rapport with Pakistan.

In June 2001, two years after Kargil, he sent an invitation to Pervez Musharraf, the army general who carried a coup when Sharif did not allow a plane in which he was travelling from China to land. Musharraf was also known to be the mastermind behind Kargil. The Vajpayee initiative was surprising, and it seemed to be in response to pressure from the United States because Washington was betting on Musharraf and there could have been no better way of lending him political legitimacy than through an India–Pakistan summit. American General Anthony Zinni had said in a TV network interview that Musharraf would be the right man to deal with in Pakistan.

The meeting was scheduled to be held in Agra. Musharraf was apparently keen to spend a night in Delhi, and he had to be accommodated in the Rashtrapati Bhavan. This could not, however, be treated as a state visit. When Home Minister L.K. Advani called on him and during their conversation reminded Musharraf about the 1993 Mumbai blasts suspect Dawood Ibrahim, the Pakistani martial law ruler contemptuously referred to it as the talk of a police sub-inspector. Vajpayee and Musharraf had a one-to-one meeting at Agra's Amarvilas hotel. There was much excitement in the liberal establishments on both sides that the two neighbours and rivals could at last reach a permanent peace agreement. The cynical argument underlying the liberal optimism was that BJP was a Hindu party and Musharraf was a military man. The compromises they made would be acceptable to their respective countries because a Hindu party like BJP would never be accused of appeasing Pakistan, and a Pakistani military ruler would not be accused of compromising with 'enemy' India. The talks broke down. Vajpayee looked harassed at the end of it, and Musharraf's face was blanched. He thought he would go back with a peace trophy much superior to what had happened between Vajpayee and Sharif in Lahore in February 1999. He could not. On the following morning, in a meeting with senior Indian editors, Musharraf had a heart-to-heart conversation, where he said that if he were to yield ground on Kashmir, then he would have to stay back in his old ancestral home in Old Delhi and he could not hope to go back to Pakistan. The press interaction was being recorded by Pakistan TV. Prannoy Roy of NDTV managed to take the CD of the recording and telecast it. It showed Musharraf in a defiant mood after the rebuff at the talks, leaving the Vajpayee government red-faced.

When Ministry of External Affairs spokesperson Nirupama Rao read out a brief, exactly a sentence, statement saying that the 'caravan of peace' would continue, there was visible anger and rage in the media, especially Pakistan media. Some of them tried to snatch the piece of paper on which the statement was written and Rao had to literally flee. It was only the next day that External Affairs Minister Jaswant Singh held a press conference and tried to explain matters. Musharraf held a press conference too in Islamabad on his return, and the Pakistani government arranged for as many Indian media persons to attend it. The Indian liberal media loved the Pakistani general-turned-martial law ruler.

Musharraf's unsuccessful India visit was followed by two major events. The first was the terrorist attacks, believed to have been carried out by Al-Qaeda—this is yet to be convincingly and conclusively established with credible forensic evidence—in New York and Washington on 11 September 2001. Because the United States was convinced that it was Al-Qaeda, it turned to Afghanistan where the Al-Qaeda leader Osama bin Laden was enjoying the protection of the Taliban regime. The Americans did not have much against the Taliban despite their cruel puritanical ways. An attempt was made through Pakistan to make the Taliban hand over Osama. The Taliban refused and the United States attacked Afghanistan. Pakistan became a key ally in the so-called global war against terrorism.

The NDA government considered it an opportune moment to prove the Indian point of Pakistan-abetted terrorism and dreamt of becoming a key US ally in the ideological war. In the BJP worldview, Pakistan was a Muslim country and the terrorism it nurtured against India was Islamic terrorism. The terrorists were of course using Islamic piety and rhetoric to unleash terror and kill innocent civilians. The Americans had no time for India because Pakistan became the important logistic base in its war in Afghanistan, which turned out to be a non-war because the Taliban regime crumbled like a cookie. But the Taliban guerrilla groups continued to indulge in terror acts in Afghanistan. In the new political set-up that emerged in Kabul after the fall of the Taliban, India was asked to participate through economic aid. India was not allowed to play a role in the political restructuring of Afghanistan and there was no room for a military role either. It was clear that Pakistan was averse to Indian troops being stationed in Afghanistan.

On 13 December 2001, a bunch of gun-wielding terrorists managed to enter the premises of Parliament House in cars. They stepped out and began to shoot haphazardly, moving towards the doors into the building. An alert watch-and-ward staff closed all the doors. The gunmen had to exchange fire with the security guards, and all of the gunmen were killed. It was seen as a terrorist act from across the border, though Pakistan had rejected the accusation. The NDA leaders felt that they had their own 11 September in the 13 December attack. Indian troops were mobilized on the border, and it sent alarm signals across Western capitals that nuclear-armed India and Pakistan are on the brink of war. Pakistan too warned of consequences if Indian troops were to cross the international border. Top US officials, British Prime Minister Tony Blair and French Prime Minister Dominique Villepin came calling to Delhi and Islamabad to avert what seemed to the Westerners as an imminent nuclear holocaust. It was clear that Pakistan was bluffing but both India and Pakistan never considered the option of reaching to the nuclear button in case there were to be a war. This point was proved in the Kargil episode of the summer of 1999. Indian troops remained mobilized for a year, and tensions eased two years later. In January 2004, India attended the South Asian Association for Regional Cooperation (SAARC) summit at Islamabad. Vajpayee and Musharraf had a separate meeting, and a joint statement was issued, where Pakistan assured that its territory would not be used for terror activities against India and India was ready for talks on all issues including that of Jammu and Kashmir. BJP felt triumphant that it was able to get the confession out of Musharraf that there was terror activity against India from groups based in Pakistan. The Indian cricket team went to Pakistan nearly after a four-year interregnum. The India–Pakistan cricket series was seen as part of the Vajpayee government's diplomatic victory. This was the last major measure that Vajpayee took on the Pakistan front.

There is an interesting arc that marks the strategic, political and diplomatic itinerary between India and Pakistan in the six years that NDA was in power. It started with the May 1998 nuclear tests, moved to the February 1999 bus ride to Lahore that Vajpayee undertook, the Kargil episode of May–July 1999, the United States intervening and forcing Pakistan to withdraw its jihadi infiltrators and India agreeing to give them a 'safe passage'. Vajpayee's invitation to General Pervez Musharraf, who had led a coup in October 1999 against the Nawaz Sharif government, came in July 2001, followed by the 11 September 2001 terror attack in the United States and the terror attack on Indian Parliament on 13 December 2001. This was followed by military confrontation sans war through 2002, and then the thaw of early 2004 when Vajpayee attended the SAARC summit in Islamabad in January 2004 and the Indian cricket team tour of Pakistan in March–April 2004.

The Pakistan factor has an important significance for a BJP-led NDA government because BJP, as the right-wing Hindu party, which had its own view of the 1947 partition of the country, was inevitably drawn into a blow hot–blow cold relationship with the arch ideological rival. Pakistan represented for BJP and for Muslim League Pakistan generation the concept of a Muslim nation, an Islamic state. Both the right-wing Hindus and right-wing Muslim leaders who created Pakistan had to come to terms with each other. BJP had to go through a dramatic series of events, of its own making and not of its own making, in dealing with Pakistan. BJP showed that it was keen to engage with Pakistan, and this desire swung to extremes from war to diplomatic warmth. Without realizing it, BJP in its first stint in office had to come to terms with the ghosts of history as it saw that history. It was a clumsy, turbulent equation, and there were enough moments of embarrassment and elation.

THE BOMB GAMBIT

On 27 May 1998, Prime Minister Atal Bihari Vajpayee told Lok Sabha:

> Sir, I rise to inform the House of momentous developments that have taken place while we were in recess. On 11 May, India successfully carried out three underground nuclear tests. Two more underground tests on 13 May completed the planned series of tests. I would like this House to join me in paying fulsome tribute to our scientists, engineers and defence personnel whose singular achievements have given us a renewed sense of national pride and self-confidence.

Vajpayee was again using his nimble wits to turn the nuclear tests to establish the political muscle of his party without sounding triumphalist. He placed the tests in perspective of India's approach to the issue of nuclear weapons. He explained as to how India was opposed to weapons of mass destruction (WMD), how India and a few Non-Aligned countries unsuccessfully tried to convince those possessing nuclear weapons to accept disarmament so that others would not go the nuclear weapons way, and how India did not sign the Non-Proliferation Treaty (NPT) of 1968 because it maintained the status quo and created a regime of nuclear apartheid where those who had nuclear weapons held on to them and the others were prevented from acquiring them. He quoted Indira Gandhi's statement in Parliament on 5 April 1968, 'We shall be guided entirely by our self-enlightenment and the consideration of national security.' Vajpayee read it mean, and rightly so, that India kept its nuclear option open. He connected this with the 1974 nuclear tests: 'Our decision not to sign the NPT was in keeping with our basic objectives. In 1974, we demonstrated our nuclear capability.' He said that there was political consensus when India did not sign the Comprehensive Nuclear-Test-Ban Treaty (CTBT) in 1996.

A feeble rationale for the tests was put forward: 'The decades of the eighties and nineties had meanwhile witnessed the gradual deterioration of our security environment as a result of nuclear and missile proliferation. In our neighbourhood nuclear weapons had increased and more sophisticated delivery systems inducted.' It would have been a credible rationalization if Vajpayee had stopped here. But he could not resist the temptation to add an issue that was the main irritant for BJP: 'In addition, India has also been the victim of externally aided and abetted terrorism, militancy and clandestine war.' This last part gave away the BJP approach that the only way to deal with Pakistan, and remotely with China, was to have the most powerful weapons. And what could be more powerful than nuclear weapons? There was also the underlying belief that nuclear weapons would act as a deterrent against those who abet terrorism and wage clandestine war. This thesis was put to test in Kargil a year later.

And here came the real assertion:

> India is now a nuclear weapon state. This is a reality that cannot be denied. It is not a conferment that we seek nor is it a status for others to grant. It is an endowment to the nation by our scientists and engineers. It is India's due, the right of one-sixth of human kind.

It seemed a strange claim to make: the right to have a nuclear bomb as an expression of self-worth. The caveats followed and that in unambiguous language: 'We do not intend to use these weapons for aggression or for mounting threats against any country, these are weapons of self-defence, to ensure that India is not subjected to nuclear threats or coercion. We do not intend to engage in an arms race.' He said that the tests were 'the minimum necessary to maintain what is an irreducible component of our national security calculus'. He also claimed that the tests—either in 1974 or in 1998—had not violated any international agreement.

This was followed by a self-imposed restraint: 'Government have already announced that India will now observe a voluntary moratorium and refrain from conducting underground nuclear test explosions.' The intriguing part is what followed, amounting to yielding to some kind of international—American?—pressure: 'We have also indicated willingness to move towards a de jure formalisation of this declaration.' A de jure obligation could only mean some kind of international agreement.

The political benefit that BJP and the Vajpayee government hoped to derive from the nuclear tests was this: 'The overwhelming support of our citizens is our source of strength. It tells us not only that this decision was right but also that our country wants a focussed leadership, which attends to their security needs.' Whatever the disagreement from the other end of the political spectrum, Vajpayee stated the right-wing credo that formed the basis of BJP's decision to go for the nuclear tests a little more than a month after coming to power.

Veteran communist leader Indrajit Gupta raised some piquant questions over the nuclear test. He said that according to the letter Vajpayee had written to US President Bill Clinton, which was leaked to the media, the threat to Indian security came from China; he referred to a government statement placed in the House in reply to Starred Question 20 (in Parliament, the starred questions are those which are taken up during the Question Hour) regarding China and quoted from it:

> In recent years, India–China relations have developed steadily. The momentum of high level dialogue has been maintained and there is a growing functional cooperation between the two countries in diverse fields. The two countries have agreed to work towards a constructive and cooperative relationship oriented towards the 21st century. The bilateral trade has reached US dollars 1.8 billion in 1997.

While pointing out that the United States could not use its nuclear weapons stockpile and that it was forced to fight 12 years to 'crush the liberation movement of the Vietnamese people', the more pointed reference from the communist leader was to the fate of the Union of Soviet Socialist Republics (USSR) which had collapsed in 1991:

> The mighty USSR got itself bankrupted by trying to chase nuclear parity with the United States and NATO. In that mad race for parity in nuclear arms, the first biggest historic casualty has been the USSR. On the other hand, Japan and Germany are considered to be the powerful States. But they do not have nuclear weapons.

The BJP leaders continued to believe that they strengthened India by making it a nuclear weapon state.

Gupta was quick to see the chink in Vajpayee's argument about voluntary moratorium:

> What exactly do you mean by this 'voluntary moratorium'...? One of the main conditionalities of the CTBT is that nuclear testing should be stopped.... If we have already unilaterally declared that we are going to go in for a voluntary moratorium, now does it mean that one of the conditionalities of the CTBT is, in fact being accepted by us by the back-door and that is the signal that we want to send out?

All that Congress's Natwar Singh could do apart from pointing to the unseemly zeal of some of Vajpayee's cabinet colleagues was to quote from the statement of Congress President Sonia Gandhi of 14 May, where she said: 'I would like to place on record, in this formal meeting of the Congress Working Committee, the pride we feel in the achievement of our nuclear scientists and engineers who are putting India's nuclear capability in the front rank.' And there was the ambiguous and ambivalent assertion in the same statement: 'The nuclear question is a national matter, not a party-run one. On this every Indian is united. The Congress Party remains committed to a nuclear-weapon-free world, non-violent world and that remains the sheet anchor of our policy.' Congress played the game with caution. It could not have denounced the tests, and it could not have acknowledged that BJP get the credit for the tests. But it was not in a position to say so.

It was P. Chidambaram of Tamil Maanila Congress who took a clear and nuanced stance. He talked about the briefing that a senior scientist deputed by the government had given to some of the political leaders, and he explained the logic of technology that was inherent in the briefing and the logic of politics that was displayed by BJP. He said:

> A few days ago, the Government was good enough to ask scientist (sic) to brief some of us on what we accomplished technically and scientifically through the tests. Some of the reasons were quite convincing. They said 'We want to validate on the field, on the ground what we had accomplished through computer simulation. We want an opportunity to pass on the next generation of scientists the knowledge and the skills involved in the simulation as well as tests.

> Sir, we have tested some nuclear devices. We pay fulsome tributes to the scientists, technologists and the engineers. We are proud that we have demonstrated our capability in this area. We are happy that these skills, acquired in 1974, have been updated and are preserved. On that, there is no quarrel. If that is all that this government wanted to do, much of the cacophony that has followed the testing would have been absent.

> This debate is about the consequences of the action that you, Mr. Prime Minister, took on 11th May and 13th May. Has the government thought through the implications of its action?'

And Chidambaram pinpointed the 'cynical, manipulated agenda behind this testing':

> Shri Jagmohan asked Shri Natwar Singh: 'What was the difference between 1974 and 1998?' The difference is this. When Shrimati Gandhi tested it, she did not utter a word

about weaponisation. You tested it and before the mushroom clouds die down, your Ministers were talking about weaponisation, about mounting warheads on missiles, about the unfinished agenda, about hot pursuit and about a fourth war.

He did not stop with the criticism. He relentlessly drove home the point and made a prescient prospective scenario:

> My fear is that from this point of time this Government can take one of the three roads. One is the road to a local limited war. I think there are people in this Government who would actively canvass to travel down this road. The other is to sign the CTBT. There are statements by a number of people including the Principal Secretary to the Prime Minister that we are willing to negotiate and accept some aspects of the CTBT. I think we should have a full scale debate on the meaning of that statement. The CTBT is not open to negotiations. It is open only to signature and 149 countries have already signed it. You can sign it up to September, 1999. It does not provide for negotiations. Whom will you negotiate with? Who has offered to negotiate CTBT with you? The second road therefore means the road which France and China took—do a few tests, acquire some political advantage and quietly sign the CTBT which means all the carefully constructed statements of the last five years that we will not sign the CTBT lie in shambles.

And the final punch was in this:

> The third road is the road to elections. Since I do not believe that you have the courage to take us to a war, since I do not believe that you have the skills to negotiate the CTBT, I am afraid you are cynically taking us to the road to elections.

The debate went into the second day on 28 May.

SP's Mulayam Singh Yadav was quite clear about BJP's decision to conduct the nuclear tests. He said that these were done to derive political mileage. He argued that BJP made no contribution to the building of nuclear capability and that it could not take credit for the tests. He accused BJP of conducting the tests in connivance with the United States, and to prove his point, he said that US President Bill Clinton did not cancel his visit to India, though the United States had imposed sanctions. He also challenged the government to impose counter-sanctions against American multinational companies doing business in India such as Pepsi and Coca-Cola. Yadav wanted to know why US President Bill Clinton was keen to visit India after he had imposed sanctions against India.

Home Minister L.K. Advani chose to quote from the 1991 Congress manifesto to show that the country was poised to exercise its choice of conducting the second nuclear test in the wake of the development and deployment of nuclear weapons by Pakistan. The part that Advani chose to quote from the manifesto was as follows:

> We are deeply concerned that Pakistan is developing the nuclear weapons. It is hoped that they will desist from this disastrous path. They have already inflicted four wars upon India. In case Pakistan persists with the development and deployment of nuclear weapons, India will be constrained to review her policy to meet the threat.

The Advani logic was that the Indian nuclear tests were necessitated by the nuclear arms programme of Pakistan.

CPI(M)'s Somnath Chatterjee cited the 1998 National Agenda of BJP-led NDA which promised to set up a national security council which would 'undertake India's first ever strategic defence review.... We will take all necessary steps and exercise all available options. Towards that end, we will revaluate the nuclear policy and exercise the option to induct nuclear weapons'. Chatterjee's criticism of the Vajpayee government was that it took the decision to conduct tests without a proper review as it had promised to do.

Chatterjee's speech was interrupted by Natwar Singh, Jaipal Reddy and Shakeel Ahmad when they wanted confirmation of the news that Pakistan 'had exploded two nuclear devices'. Minister of Information and Broadcasting and Minister of Communications Sushma Swaraj said, 'I will let you know the authentic news within five minutes....' She came back and told the House:

> Mr Speaker, Sir, just now I am informed that today Pakistan has conducted two tests at 3.30 p.m. The news to this effect was received by Hon'ble Prime Minister also. We are collecting the facts. I will give detailed statement of facts in the House. This information is correct and flash news has been telecast on Doordarshan that at 3.30 p.m. Pakistan has conducted two tests.

Chatterjee said, 'The Prime Minister has come. May I continue? Does he want to make a statement?'

Vajpayee said, 'Would he like to complete first?'

Chatterjee said, 'No. He should categorically state whether the information is correct or not.'

Then Vajpayee stated,

> Mr Speaker, Sir, according to the information received, Pakistan has conducted two nuclear tests. Detailed information is not yet available. I am collecting the facts, and will place them in the House. If it is true that Pakistan has conducted the nuclear test, it vindicates the policy adopted by India in this regard....

Chatterjee resumed his speech, and he concluded his speech saying, 'Sir, Shri Vajpayee is a good student of history. After the 1974 blasts came the Emergency, and 1977 was the end of that Government. So, do not be under an euphoria.'

Vajpayee in his concluding remarks just said that in 1974, he was in the Opposition but he supported the nuclear tests. He said that at that time, Indira Gandhi did not consult the Opposition but that did not prevent him from standing with the government.

XIII Chapter

LOVE AND WAR

On 15 March 1999, in his reply to the Motion of Thanks to the President's Address, Vajpayee told the Lok Sabha about his trip to Lahore and the Lahore Declaration. He explained it as a simple bilateral visit:

> I got an opportunity to go to Pakistan at the invitation of Pakistan Prime Minister. I took advantage of the bus service which was starting the same day. I am happy that our talks went well. In the Lahore Declaration and in the Memorandum of Understanding prepared by the foreign secretaries, some new measures were announced. Now, both India and Pakistan are nuclear states. There is no other way than to live together in peace.

He justified the nuclear explosions as having introduced an element of balance of power or the balance of terror, and he cited the parallel of the Cold War for the long peace between the two superpowers, the United States and the Soviet Union: 'If there was no balance of power or balance of terror during the days of the cold war, the odds could have been in favour of one party and it could have committed excesses.' He also narrated that the Pakistan prime minister (Nawaz Sharif) wanted to know why India undertook the nuclear tests on that particular day. When he asked for the reason behind the question, the Pakistani prime minister 'laughed and said that our action coincided with the lowest ever foreign exchange reserves position in Pakistan'.

He also mentioned:

> When I was in Lahore, the news came of a massacre taking place in Rajouri the same day. I took up the matter

immediately with the Pakistan Prime Minister and told him that 'if this process of killing innocent people did not stop, the bus of our friendship would come to a halt before their corpses'.

He made it clear that the Lahore Declaration honours 'the Shimla Agreement both in the letter and the spirit'.

There was, however, a dramatic change in the fortune of the BJP-led coalition government of 13 parties at the end of March. When AIADMK walked out of the coalition, Congress with other Opposition parties met President K.R. Narayanan and staked claim to form the government. The president asked Vajpayee to prove his majority in Lok Sabha. He moved a confidence motion on 15 April, and at the end of a two-day debate on 17 April, the 13-month Vajpayee government was voted out by a margin of one vote. The BJP-led coalition government had 269 votes; the Opposition had 270.

The ostensible reason for AIADMK General Secretary J. Jayalalithaa to walk out of the Vajpayee government was the dismissal of Chief of the Naval Staff Admiral Vishnu Bhagwat by Defence Minister George Fernandes. Fernandes told Lok Sabha during his intervention on 16 April in the debate that he met the general secretary of AIADMK at the Taj Mahal Hotel in the capital, but that he did not show her any file as was rumoured in the media. Fernandes said that he went into the hotel empty-handed and came out empty-handed, implying that he could not get an assurance from Jayalalithaa that she would come back to the government. And he said,

> If you want to know the reason for removal of the Navy Chief then discussion must be held in such a way that confidential matters need to be disclosed publically. The discussion should take place in front of such people who know about security matters. The nation will face trouble if we disclose everything publically. So, I, the Prime Minister, the Minister of Home Affairs had expressed such views to the hon. Speaker of the House.

Fernandes also blamed Bhagwat for leaking Ministry of Defence papers to the media and quoted from the letter dated 30 October 1990 of Vice Admiral S. Jain, FOC-in-C Western Command to the then Naval Chief, where he made adverse remarks against Bhagwat's personality:

> Bhagwat has made malicious and false accusations ... is a disgruntled officer who is also mentally unbalanced. He is schizophrenic and needs psychiatric help ... has developed a sinister information gathering net-work within the service and the Government for ulterior motives ... have been spying on his superiors, subordinates, peers ... has not hesitated to tap telephones ... has rifled through desks of others.

Dr Subramanian Swamy, the Janata Party member from Madurai, stuck back when his turn came. He also spoke for AIADMK:

> The withdrawal of support by the AIADMK's leader was necessitated because the leader, Kumari Jayalalita found that this Government gravely jeopardised our national security and demoralised our Armed Forces by the reckless dismissal of Admiral Vishnu Bhagwat. The Admiral was dismissed on 30th of December (1998) and as early as the second of January (1999), the leader of the AIADMK issued a public statement on the issue.

He also accused Fernandes of being pro-LTTE, and he cited chapter and verse to trace the details of why Bhagwat thought that the defence minister was unfit to be defence minister. He said that Fernandes was keen to humiliate Bhagwat because LTTE hated Bhagwat for intercepting their number two man, Kittu, on the high seas in 1995. 'The second reason for Admiral Bhagwat's conviction was that Mr Fernandes was a national security risk of which he had given many documentation (sic).'

BJP and its allies came back to power. BJP had 182 seats, 1 seat more than in the outgoing Parliament of March 1999. And the Parliament met in October 1999. In the intervening summer, the Kargil episode occurred. It was the first big conflagration between the two countries after they had tested nuclear devices and they had declared that they were nuclear weapon states. When it came out into the open that the Pakistani irregulars, militants or jihadis were occupying the mountain heights and the Indian Army was launching a counter-offensive to recapture them, the BJP-led caretaker government was on the back foot. In an interesting development, the Army had been allowed to go up to the front lines and talk to soldiers in the bunkers before they went into the operation. It was something new. It evoked sentiments of patriotism in the country as all wars did in India. The government had also decided to send the bodies of the dead soldiers to their villages and towns, and their funerals were televised. This was India's first TV war. The world had seen its first one in January 1991 when the world TV channels showed the attack of the US planes on Baghdad.

In the Motion of Thanks to the President's Address, CPI's Indrajit Gupta raised the issue. Speaking on 29 October, Gupta referred to the Kargil issue. Vajpayee's Lahore visit became the inevitable reference point, and Gupta made the point:

> Now, I do not know whether it is a fact that because of Shri Vajpayee's famous bus ride to Lahore and the fact which some are saying that he was, perhaps taken in by the Pakistani Prime Minister's professions of friendship that had the effect of lulling our vigilance and the Prime Minister and his other Members of the Government naturally could not imagine that within a few days such an incursion could take place which obviously could or must have been prepared long before.

He pointed out that the government woke up to the fact of the incursion

> only after the Pakistani shelling began, aimed at disrupting the Srinagar–Leh road which was down below, which was obviously their main target which they started shelling from above, that the Government seems to have woken

up and were taken by surprise and asked this question as to how this was happening.

He quoted Lt General Shankar Prasad's statement blaming the Research and Analysis Wing (R&AW), and the director of the Intelligence Bureau's statement that he warned the Army 'that preparations are going on for some sort of mischief'.

Gupta was angry that the government did not feel the need to call Rajya Sabha to debate the Kargil situation. He said that during Hitler's blitzkrieg of 1941 when London was being bombarded, the House of Commons met every night and 'Sir Winston Churchill had to face the Parliament and come out with facts as they were known.' He went on to argue:

> In our case half the Parliament was functioning. The Rajya Sabha was in existence, the Lok Sabha was not there. But curiously enough, the Government felt that any discussion or debate in the Rajya Sabha would be harmful and there was no need for it.... As far as I know, legally or constitutionally, the Parliament of India does not consist of only one of the two Houses. Both the Houses and the President constitute the Parliament.

Home Minister L.K. Advani replied to the Motion of Thanks to President's Address because Vajpayee was indisposed. Advani felt that it would have been better if Vajpayee had replied. He referred to the fact that the government had won the mandate in the election: 'The manner in which he successfully led the country during the last one and a half years is the main factor behind this mandate.' He also noted the fact that the Vajpayee government was not seeking a confidence motion as it did in 1996 and 1998 because it had a clear majority, and that is why the president did not ask the new government to seek a vote of confidence, which H.D. Deve Gowda in 1996, V.P. Singh in 1989 and P.V. Narasimha Rao in 1991 had to seek because they led minority governments. And he said:

> I agree that the people's mandate is in favour of Stable Government. I remember that while framing our manifesto,

we have stated the reasons for the formation of N.D.A.: 'NDA came into being because of an historic need and realisation among us that our young democracy cannot bear the fits and tremors of frequent elections which will undermine the people's faith in the democratic process.'

Referring to the Kargil issue, Advani objected to the interpretation that it was American pressure that forced Pakistan's infiltrators to withdraw.

> Almost the whole area of Kargil that had been invaded had been cleared by our jawans. It was the last phase when the Pakistani Prime Minister had visited Washington on the invitation of United States President Mr. Clinton. He committed over there that the remaining intruders will retreat.... Only some intruders were left by that time.

Advani then explained what the government did once it came to know about the infiltration:

> According to my information, the Government came to know about intrusion on 8 May and since then the Government had been regularly taking decisions. I am not aware that the Cabinet Committee on Security had met so many times in the past as it had met in that one and a half month. Many a time the meetings took place twice a day. Not only defence people but other people were also there. It had three heads of defence forces. The continuous discussion on this was held, and even small decisions taken at that time had shown good results.

One of those decisions for which Advani took credit was showing the funerals of the dead soldiers on TV. He acknowledged that the earlier practice was to cremate or bury the soldier on the battlefield, and the remains and belongings were handed over to the family.

> This time it was decided the dead bodies of the martyrs should be sent to their native villages and their funeral should take place with full honour and respect.... The coffins of the martyrs were shown on television. Somebody

objected to it being shown on television. They said you may send it to villages but do not show it on television. But I think that this decision has kindled the feeling of patriotism.... They had proven beneficial for the country. Through television, the martyrdom of the Indian soldiers reached every nook and corner of the country....

He argued that unlike the earlier wars of 1947, 1965 and 1971, where there was victory on the battlefield and defeat on the diplomatic front, this time around India scored militarily as well as in the international arena. He was referring to the UN declaration of ceasefire after the 1947 war, the Tashkent Agreement after the 1965 war when India returned occupied territories including Haji Pir and the Simla Agreement after the 1971 war when India returned the more than 90,000 soldiers captured in Dhaka. Rajesh Pilot argued that 1971 was different, that it was a full-fledged war and that 1971 cannot be compared to Kargil. Advani argued that though there was no declaration of war, the challenge was no less than a war. Mani Shankar Aiyar argued that it was because of Simla Agreement that Kashmir did not become an international issue. Advani agreed but went on to give his own analysis of why Pakistan mounted an attack in Kargil:

I understand that Pakistan has attacked Kargil because they misjudged our system. They felt that recently the opposition had pulled down the Government, and in that condition 'this Government will be totally isolated'. They misjudged our system; they misjudged our people; and they also misjudged our Government.

Advani finally came up with the BJP dilemma of dealing with Pakistan, and he explained it in the context of Vajpayee's Lahore visit:

While mentioning the Lahore visit of Shri Atal Bihari Vajpayee, many friends have said that he was unaware of the plot being orchestrated behind his back. I agree that all this might had been planned at that time. There is no doubt about it and I am not denying it. But I am also of the view that the Lahore visit of Shri Atal Bihari Vajpayee served a great purpose. Earlier, it was publicised all over the world that all other political parties, except Bharatiya Janata Party want friendly ties with Pakistan. This party wants that the relations with Pakistan should always remain tense ... that is not true. Sir, this decision of Shri Atal Bihari Vajpayee disabused the minds of millions in the world, many countries in the world.

He drew the right, if obvious, conclusion:

The fall out of Kargil war is that it has strengthened democracy in our country. The Government which came into being is more stable. But what is the fall out of it in Pakistan? It is a sharp contrast of what has happened here. In Pakistan, democracy is undermined, and the military is ruling the country.

GENERAL BLUFFS, AGRA BLUES

In the last week of May 2001, Prime Minister Atal Bihari Vajpayee shot off a letter to President Pervez Musharraf to come to India for talks. There was no specific agenda. This was the first major diplomatic initiative after the Lahore high and Kargil low. It would appear that BJP wanted to do something on the Pakistan front, which would leave behind a permanent impact. It took a month to fix the dates and the venue. It was decided to hold the talks in Agra, which was the Mughal capital for about 125 years before Shah Jahan shifted to Delhi, and which had masterly Mughal monuments like the Taj Mahal in the vicinity, the abandoned poetic city of Fatehpur Sikri and the majestic tomb of Akbar at Sikandra. While Indira Gandhi met Pakistani Prime Minister Zulfiqar Ali Bhutto in the colonial hill resort of Shimla after India's military victory in the Bangladesh War, Vajpayee chose Agra in the plains. It is possible to speculate that Vajpayee chose the seat of Mughal and Muslim glory to speak to the military ruler of Pakistan. This aspect was never mentioned in the endless discussions on the only private English language TV news channel of NDTV, nor in the lengthy editorial comments in the newspapers. Looking back, it seems that Agra seemed the right place for a right-wing BJP with its own view of subcontinental history to deal with Pakistan, an ostensible country of Muslims. It is something like the Marathas in the late 18th century wanting to deal with the Afghans or Sikhs or the East India Company from the then Mughal seat of power in Delhi.

The liberals in India, who were generally averse to BJP and who were not reconciled to the fact that BJP was heading a coalition government, were swept off their feet by Vajpayee's gesture to talk with Pakistan. They argued with a combined sense of cynicism and realism that the best way to solve the problems between India and Pakistan was for a Hindu party like BJP to talk to the military rulers of Pakistan so that hardliners on both sides would find it difficult to reject whatever agreements were made between the two right-wing elements. There was a strange euphoria in the secular circles of Delhi, and BJP felt satisfied that it had won over the internal critics.

Pervez Musharraf played the part of the plain-speaking gruff soldier to the hilt, appearing to scorn ceremony and custom, rules and formalities. He wanted to talk straight and clinch an agreement. If Vajpayee and BJP wanted to win their place in history through a breakthrough agreement, Musharraf too was keen to seal his place in Pakistani politics, if not in history, that he had managed to do a decent deal with India.

The Vajpayee–Musharraf talks in Agra attracted the most dense and intense media coverage from the two countries. When the protracted talks, including the one-to-one between Vajpayee and Musharraf, ended, there was no breakthrough, and Musharraf seemed crestfallen and angry. The liberals in the Indian media blamed the hardliner and Home Minister L.K. Advani for not letting Musharraf have his way, and it was said that Vajpayee would have been lenient and the positive outcome would have been good for relations between the two countries.

What transpired during the talks, and what was the criticism of the Opposition parties, on the Agra summit came out in the discussion in Lok Sabha held from 24 July to 6 August. Vajpayee made a suo motu statement on 24 July, where he gave a summary of the Agra initiative, the failure to get out a joint statement, and that Musharraf had invited him to visit Pakistan and that he had accepted it, as did Minister of External Affairs Jaswant Singh from his Pakistani counterpart Abdul Sattar.

Vajpayee said, 'At the retreat in Agra on July 15 and 16, President Musharraf and I had extensive one-to-one talks for over five hours. We also had talks at the delegation level.' He explained:

> Eventually, however, we had to abandon the quest for a joint document mainly because of Pakistan's insistence on the settlement of Jammu and Kashmir issue, as a precondition for the normalisation of relations.... My Cabinet colleagues and I were unanimously of the view that our basic principles cannot be sacrificed for the sake of a joint document.

And he added: 'Though we could not conclude a joint document in Agra, we did achieve a degree of understanding.' He ended on an apologetic note: 'Let me add—we are not looking for propaganda advantage or seeking to score debating point. We will engage in quiet, serious diplomacy.'

Opening the debate, Mulayam Singh Yadav wanted to know the reason for sending an invitation to Musharraf, contrary to his (Vajpayee's) earlier stance that there would be no talks until 'Pakistan stops and puts a check on cross border terrorism and a democratically elected government is set up in Pakistan'. He pointed out the statement of Musharraf that even as Mukti Bahini helped in the liberation of Bangladesh, 'jehadis in Kashmir are fighting for independence.'

It was the Congress deputy leader in Lok Sabha Madhavrao Scindia who described the Agra outcome in clear terms: 'The Agra Summit has left the country confused.' And he delineated the confusion:

> The first reaction of the hon. Minister of External Affairs was: 'In the Summit, we have made progress. We have embarked on a journey which is going to lead us to destination called peace.' Two days later, the Foreign Ministry disowns Agra as 'a bad dream'. Then, one day later, it is announced that the hon. Foreign Minister has accepted Mr. Sattar's invitation to visit Pakistan, 'to pick up threads from General Musharraf's visit'.

The Congress leader, in his own quiet way, demolished the government's hare-brained initiative:

▌ The Government suddenly woke up one day and like a Budget traveller, they took the flight to Agra without even checking properly what they had taken in their bags. Mr Prime Minister, you did not seem to be prepared for the journey that you had chosen to embark on. Agra was one of the rare summits which will go down in history as one where confusion on the very agenda was allowed to prevail till the eve of the Summit.

Scindia summed up the Agra summit effectively and briefly:

▌ As far as the Summit is concerned, we lost before the Summit, we lost during the Summit and we have lost after the Summit. We lost before the Summit because General Musharraf did not want an agenda. This was his ploy. If there had been a structured agenda, he could not have kept merely pushing 'Kashmir'–Jammu and Kashmir–in the discussion. He did not want an agenda. We gave in. We lost during the Summit because they were more articulate and more communicative. We have lost after the summit because of the international impression that the Cabinet is divided, and that the country was confused.

BJP's senior leader and chief whip Vijay Kumar Malhotra argued that Musharraf had to go back empty-handed and that the prime minister did not yield ground and that was a victory in itself. 'He is the first Prime Minister in the last fifty years who did not compromise with the conditions of Pakistan and Shri Musharraf had to go empty-handed,' explained Malhotra. He also accepted that there was pressure from other political parties in the country and other countries to hold talks with Pakistan.

Malhotra explained:

▌ Pakistan in the entire world was making a propaganda that they were ready to hold talks but India was not ready. Even the Congress Party and CPI (M) people were pressurising to hold talks. So when all the political parties of India as also other countries have been insisting that

India should hold talks with Pakistan, our hon. Prime Minister took the initiative and got ready to hold talks, but not on the conditions of Pakistan. What can we do if Pakistan had said that they do not want to fix any agenda?

He concluded tamely saying, 'My opinion is that the circumstances were such that no solid ground could be created, due to which the Summit failed, and this is our biggest achievement.'

Mani Shankar Aiyar of Congress countered the BJP view with biting sarcasm:

> Is it a Machiavellian technique, calling the President of Pakistan in order to send him back empty-handed? If so, I think, this House is entitled to know, in all honesty that the Prime Minister's strategy was to engineer a failure of the Summit. We cannot have it both ways. We cannot have the failure of a Summit projected as the success of the Prime Minister.

Surprising support for Vajpayee and the government came from Indian Union Muslim League (IUML)'s G.M. Banatwala.

> It was a partial success because of the restoration of the process of dialogue. From the very beginning—I had made it very clear in the meeting of the party leaders called by the hon. Prime Minister—we never looked upon the Indo-Pak Summit as result-oriented. It would be naïve and folly to have so considered the Summit. We always insisted that the correct perception was to expect the Summit to be not result-oriented but process-oriented. In this sense, the Summit was a partial success.

Minister of External Affairs Jaswant Singh tried to give out as much of the detail as he could. It is certain that he did not reveal all. The problems were many, and most importantly it was the personality of Pervez Musharraf that became the problem. The Indian government could do nothing but to concede on small points of his temperament and fancy, and they had to resist his big point on Jammu and Kashmir. Musharraf seemed determined to solve the Kashmir question before going on to other less intransigent ones. The minister pointed out:

> There was no prepared text on Pakistan side. The notes ... by the visiting head of Government/State ... were made on the table while the Indian Prime Minister was presenting. It was that kind of a situation. That was the kind of military simplicism if I might put it as politely as I can. The President of Pakistan never fights shy of extolling the virtues of soldierly qualities. He is not at all hesitant or inhibited in putting across that he has the attribute of soldierly directness.

Singh said that the Agra summit was conceived as a retreat, where the two leaders could have a one-to-one meeting 'so that complex and intricate issues' were addressed 'in privacy'. Initially, the Indian government wanted the retreat to be held in Goa. But this had to be dropped because a 'direct request of the visiting dignitary, directly to the Prime Minister was made, "I must come to Delhi." It is not possible for the host, thereafter, to say, no, you cannot come to Delhi.' This was followed by another request that he (Musharraf) wanted to spend a night in Delhi.

The Agra retreat was fixed for 15 and 16 July after Musharraf spent the day and night of 14 July in Delhi. Singh explained: 'The 15th afternoon ended with an agreed text of a joint statement between India and Pakistan giving an account of the discussions till then. On the 15th evening, before the Banquet by the Governor of U.P., that Joint Statement was to be issued.' Singh said that a request was to depute a team of Pakistan officials who would sit with their Indian counterparts and prepare the draft of the joint statement. Singh then gave the detailed account:

> The officials from Pakistan side would just not sit with our officials because they had no directions; they had no instructions and they had no document. It was after the banquet was over—by now we have reached 11 o'clock at night on the 15th—finally, at 11 o'clock at night, Pakistan

officials said that they were then ready to sit with us. This was on the 15th evening.

They prepared a draft by 4:30 on the morning of 16 July. Then Singh made an interesting passing remark: 'There must have been many pieces of paper on which I attempted to correct all kinds of things from the quality of Punjabi English and grammar to punctuation.'

There were many square brackets—'Square brackets are areas where there is no agreement,' Singh told the House—and Vajpayee wanted Singh to be present even though it was supposed to be a one-to-one meeting so that he (Singh) could explain the square brackets. At this point, Pakistani Foreign Minister Abdul Sattar was also called in. 'The 12.30 deadline could not be met. It kept on prolonging. Every effort was made. What was holding it up? What was holding it up was what the Prime Minister had clearly said—Pakistan's continued emphasis that everything is dependent on Jammu and Kashmir.'

The initiative taken by Vajpayee and which led to the Agra summit did not work. The Vajpayee–Musharraf meeting that proved fruitful was on the sidelines of SAARC in Islamabad on 6 January 2004. The key paragraph of the joint statement from the Vajpayee government's point of view after the Agra setback of July 2001 was as follows:

> Prime Minister Vajpayee said that in order to take forward and sustain the dialogue process, violence, hostility and terrorism must be prevented. President Musharraf reassured Prime Minister Vajpayee that he will not permit any territory under Pakistan's control to be used to support terrorism in any manner.

Musharraf and Pakistan were able to hold on to their Kashmir card in the following paragraph of the statement:

> To carry the process of normalisation forward, the President of Pakistan and the Prime Minister of India agreed to commence the process of the composite

dialogue in February 2004. The two leaders are confident that the resumption of the composite dialogue will lead to peaceful settlement of all bilateral issues, including Jammu and Kashmir, to the satisfaction of both sides.

In May 2004, BJP-led NDA demitted office after their defeat in the Lok Sabha elections. And that brought to an end what BJP could do in leaving its mark on India–Pakistan relations.

XV
Chapter

MODI'S INFERNO

If the Kargil episode was India's first televised war, then the 2002 Gujarat communal violence was the country's first televised riot. It started with the burning of the bogie of the Sabarmati Express on the outskirts of the Godhra railway station, killing about 59 passengers of S6. This was followed by the retaliatory killings of Muslims all over Gujarat, which lasted for four days.

The Gujarat riots were connected to the Ayodhya issue. The kar sevaks, volunteers mostly belonging to VHP, were returning from Ayodhya. According to reports, the kar sevaks harassed a Muslim girl in Godhra railway station, and the local Muslim mob attacked S6 when the train pulled out of the station and halted on the outskirts.

It was a test for the BJP government in the state led by Chief Minister Narendra Modi for two reasons. First, how would an unapologetic Hindu party like BJP deal with Hindu–Muslim riots when it is in power? Second, did Modi, a Hindu hardliner even by BJP standards, take an impartial stand and deal with the perpetrators of the violence, whether they were Hindus or Muslims? There was also the issue whether secular parties like the Congress, which were accused by BJP and the others for being pro-Muslims and pro-minorities, were outraged at the burning of Hindus at the hands of Muslim arsonists in Godhra? These were the issues that formed the crux of the debate that took place in the Lok Sabha on 11 March 2002, a week after the violence was brought under control.

An hour before the discussion on Gujarat riots, which started at 12:24 PM, former Prime Minister H.D. Deve Gowda raised the issue of kar sevaks gathering at Ayodhya in large numbers, and referred to Prime Minister Vajpayee's assurance that 'they (the kar sewaks) will abide by the court verdict.' Gowda persisted:

> Sir, on the one side, the Prime Minister says that they are going to abide by the court verdict and on the other side necessary preparations are being made to allow all the kar sevaks to assemble there. The hon. Minister, Uma Bharati also says that they are not going to stop the construction of the temple there at any cost.

Mulayam Singh Yadav then intervened, speaking about Ayodhya and about Godhra, and referring to the serious situation in Ayodhya.

Vajpayee clarified the issue:

> Shri Mulayam Singhji is not fair enough when he says that Ayodhya is burning.... (interruptions) Now there is peace in Ayodhya. The situation is fully under control. I want to inform the House about the arrangements which have been made. At present, 41 companies of CRPF, 23 companies of PAC, 400 constables and 100 sub-inspectors of UP police are deputed in Ayodhya.

Vajpayee explained that the Shri Ram Janmabhoomi Nyas has written to the government, seeking permission to perform *yagya* (fire ritual) on the undisputed land which is under the control of the government. The important development according to the prime minister was as follows:

> Shri Ram Janam Bhumi Nyas had also informed the Government that it is ready to accept the decision of court in regard to Ayodhya.... A new turn has come in Ayodhya dispute. Till now, Hindu Parishad and its other affiliated institutions used to say that this matter could not [be] settled in court because it is matter of loyalty. We rejected it.... Ram Janam Bhumi Nyas has announced that it is bound to the decision of the court even if it goes against it.... The announcement of 'Nyas' that they will accept decision of court is an important announcement. I urge the

House as well as the citizens that they should accept the importance of this announcement and shall give their cooperation to solve this problem.

Priya Ranjan Dasmunsi, the Congress leader who opened the debate at 12:25 PM under Rule 193, first referred to the developments in Ayodhya and the letter that his Party President Sonia Gandhi had written to the prime minister on 22 February expressing concern over the developments in Ayodhya and requested him to convene an all-party meeting and that the prime minister did convene a meeting on 26 February.

Then he came to the issue of the Godhra and post-Godhra violence. Dasmunsi was eager to prove that Party President Sonia Gandhi was the first to condemn the burning of passengers at Godhra and that even Parliamentary Affairs Minister Pramod Mahajan acknowledged that Sonia Gandhi's was the first statement on Godhra. Dasmunsi said:

> The incident of Godhra took place on 27th morning. The massacre took place between 7.45 a.m. and 9 a.m.–the horrendous incident, the dastardly incident, the ghastly incident, the most condemnable incident. No words are enough to condemn what happened in Godhra. And our leader, Shrimati Sonia Gandhi, on the same day, issued a statement condemning the incident of Godhra which was not only reported in the media but also I am thankful to the hon. Parliamentary Affairs Minister, Shri Pramod Mahajan, that in the Speaker's Chamber he also acknowledged that the first statement came from Shrimati Sonia Gandhi condemning the issue of Godhra.

Then he went on to point out the tardy response of the government to the situation in Gujarat. He said that Congress wanted the government to make a statement on the morning of 28. But the home minister was not ready to make a statement. Dasmunsi set out the timeline:

> The Godhra incident took place between 8 and 9 in the morning on 27th of February. On 28th, immediately after

the Budget—the time was between 1.30 p.m. and 1.35 p.m.; I remember the time—the Home Minister of India was not in a position to make an official statement in the House about the incident and he had to say: 'I am trying to get more details and I shall come back tomorrow.' Tomorrow means the 1st of March. On 28th, when the Budget was being read out, Gujarat was in flames. On 28th, when the Budget speech was over, the massacre of Gujarat was in a desperate situation. Yet, the Home Minister could not make a statement on the previous day's incident forget what was the on-going development in Gujarat on that day.... The Hon. Prime Minister is here. His appeal to the nation came on the 2nd March evening on television.

Dasmunsi narrated three things which reflected the Hindu majoritarian mood and the sense of helplessness among Muslims.

I was shocked to hear on the day of the incident of Godhra, in this Parliament a slogan was shouted 'The person who favours Hindus will rule the country.' And I heard that same slogan on the streets of Ahmedabad on 3rd March when hon. Member Shri Kamal Nath led a delegation with us to Ahmedabad.

The second was what 80-year-old tailor Maqbool Ansari at the V.S. Hospital told Dasmunsi: 'Please do one thing for us, tell the Government and Hon. President of India to withdraw our voting right.' The third incident he witnessed was in his own words:

The most shocking incident in the city civil hospital. Till 10 o'clock in the morning, I say this with responsibility, that no injured Muslim patient was allowed to be admitted in the hospital. People with open swords were standing there and saying that 'The person who is Muslim will not be admitted in the hospital....'

He referred to Defence Minister George Fernandes telling the *Times of India* that when he (Fernandes) asked during the 1969 riots then Chief Minister Hiten Desai and his cabinet colleagues whether they could not come out on the streets and control the riots, they did and that Indulal Yajnik led the morcha, and raised the question:

> Was it not possible for Shri Narendra Modi–who was a pracharak and who led the sadhus and the sanyasis to the Millennium summit and I saw him in the streets of New York with the sadhus and sanyasis who were later addressed by the hon. Prime Minister in a VHP gathering– to do such a thing in Gujarat?

Dasmunsi argued that Home Minister L.K. Advani assumed that Gujarat Chief Minister Narendra Modi would handle the crisis and there was no need to send the Army, and that Advani was proved wrong when Modi asked for help from the Army. He ended his speech pointing to Modi's ineptness and inability to deal with the situation:

> It is a fact that Shri Modi, the Chief Minister, on the 28th evening issued a statement saying: 'It was revenge, what can I do? I am trying to control.' Why should the Chief Minister use the word revenge? Let the VHP say that they were taking revenge. Or let the RSS say that. Chief Minister is a Constitutional office. Can a Constitutional authority feel like that?

Earlier in his speech, Dasmunsi made the devastating confession about the Congress government's failure under Narasimha Rao to protect the Babri Masjid in Ayodhya. He said:

> Sir, 27th is over; 28th is over. Till 6.30 in the evening your Government, both in the Centre and in State, did not act. I know my Left friends will say this is what happened on 6th December, 1992 when Kalyan Singh was not doing his duty or the Prime Minister was also not doing his duty. Yes, I confess, bowing my head before this Parliament, that our Prime Minister did not act in time. He paid for it. We paid for it. We have learnt the lesson. One has to make a journey

for learning lesson from history. That is what is India. That is what Gandhiji taught. Gandhiji said, 'I am not a great man. I have done sin in my life, please hate that. My life is my message. Please forget and forgive the part of my life which could not stand by the people.'

Home Minister Advani's reply was measured, and he tried his best to defend the administration both at the Centre and in the state. Advani pleaded that these happenings are a shame and a blot. He said, 'Either in the case of Godhra or in the case of Ahmedabad or in the case of Rajkot, the whole thing is a series of happenings which certainly—as the hon. Prime Minister has said—are a shame for us. They are a blot for us.' He once again revealed the vulnerability of BJP in matters of communalism:

> For us in Government, it is a blot or it is a stain also because when we came to power four years back, one of the principal misgivings in the minds of many was that under this rule minorities would be unsafe, the minorities would feel insecure. It was our earnest effort to see that this kind of misgiving and apprehension is removed.

The government was confused and was faltering in its response to the outbreak of riots in Gujarat. BJP leaders wanted to be seen to be doing the right things. They did not want to be accused of being communal. And this was reflected in Advani's reply to the debate:

> I have with me the statement that I had prepared immediately after the happening and I was to make it in the House, but somehow, I could not make it in this House. In that statement, I have not only referred to Godhra, but said that no words can adequately condemn the acts of horrendous violence that Gujarat has witnessed in the past few days.

Advani had always tried to retain his rational tone because he was very much aware that he could not pull off the emotional, rhetorical turns of phrases that Vajpayee did. So Advani, in his reasonable tone, stated:

> Today, I would say that in Gujarat, after all that has happened, there would be a sense of insecurity even though there may be peace and there may be no incident. These are the matters which have to be considered, and I said that the torching of Sabarmati Express in Godhra in which 58 persons were burnt alive and the setting afire of a residential building in Ahmedabad in which 38 persons, including a former hon. Member of this House, Shri Ehsan Jafri and his family were burnt alive, are heinous crimes which shocked the nation. This was the statement that I had prepared. That was my immediate reaction.

Then he went on to defend the state police:

> I do not know of a single riot in the past in which the police in firing has killed 100 persons. If the total number of persons killed during these tragedies is around 600 or slightly more, one hundred people have been killed in police firing. Someone said in the other House and even here also, perhaps Shri Mulayam Singh Yadav said that the police was asked that if it is one community, you fire at them and if it is other community, then you turn your eyes away, you close your eyes. Otherwise I would not have referred to Hindus and Muslims. So, I asked them to check up that these 100 persons who have died in police firing, what is their communal break up and I was told they are 60 Hindus and 40 Muslims. Now, I am not giving this explanation as anything except to say that I cannot, in honesty, accuse the police either of passivity or collusion. There may be instances where they failed to perform their duty.

Advani turned to the issue of deployment of security forces:

> The Chief Minister of Gujarat spoke to me on the first day, on the 27th saying that he needed para-military forces. I checked up and found that the Rapid Action Force (RAF), which is the CRPF unit trained specifically to deal with communal situations, had four companies present there

and I said: 'Send them immediately.' These four companies were posted in Ahmedabad to assist the State Government on the 27th itself. On the 28th I sought further companies so that apart from those four Rapid Action Force companies, three BSF companies and two CISF companies were also sent there.

He referred to the issue of asking the Army:

> Also in the morning, the Chief Minister contacted the local Army unit, and they said, 'we have no Army unit here; we cannot give any Army assistance. You will have to speak to the Centre.' Around 2.30 or so, he spoke to me. He said: 'we would need Army assistance. We will not be able to do it.' Then, I spoke to the hon. Prime Minister and to the Cabinet Secretary. In the meanwhile, he also spoke to the Defence Minister.

He explained the difficulty:

> You must realise that we are in a situation where the bulk of the Army has been deployed on the frontiers. For the first time in the Indian history, simply to send the Army, to assist the State Government in a law and order situation—which normally everybody knows that the Army does not relish very much—a special meeting of the Cabinet Committee on Security had to be convened by the Prime Minister.

Once again, the rational Advani gave the details about how the decision to send the Army was taken:

> I also felt at a point that what was the need to hold a meeting of special Cabinet Committee on Security. After all, the Prime Minister is there, the Defence Minister is there, and when the Chief Minister has requested for Army assistance, we should immediately order. But after participating in that meeting, I felt that the Prime Minister did the right thing to convene the CCS. In that meeting, even the three Chiefs of the Armed Forces were there.

They presented their point of view and then said, 'It is for the Government to decide.' And, the Government had decided that the Army had to go. Then, not only the Army had to go but because I had to make a Statement in the House the next day, therefore, the hon. Prime Minister thought it proper that now when the Army was going, let the Defence Minister also go, and the Defence Minister was deputed.... I do not want to score any debating points. But I can tell you that in the matter of Army use, the Government has acted very responsibly, and very expeditiously. There has been no delay of any kind.

He also explained as to why the phrase 'Army is on the standby' was used even though the Army was deployed:

> When it was said that the Army has been asked to stand by the Leader of Opposition, through Dr. Manmohan Singh conveyed to me that why can it not be said that the Army has been deployed? I said that it would be deployed. It is being sent for that. But it is a phrase that they had themselves chosen earlier. They had suggested to use this phrase. We conceded to that and we said: 'All right, we will say that the Army has been asked to stand by.' And, we used that phrase, though it was sent. It has been picked up from the distant area and transported by a plane.

Advani also said that the police had in many instances managed to save the lives of many Muslims, including at the Gulberg Housing Society where a former Congress MP Ehsan Jafri and his family members were killed. He told the House:

> I have with me a long list of incidents in Ahmedabad itself and in other places also, where the police has done a remarkable work in rescuing members of the minority community. It includes the incident in Gulberg Society in Chamanpura where Shri Ehsan Jafri and his family were burnt, and where 19 houses were the target of petrol bombs, acid bulbs, and burning rugs. The mob set fire to all the 19 houses, one of them belonging to Shri Jafri and

his family. Braving mob fury and missiles-type of attacks, the police under the Joint Police Commissioner, DCP rushed to the site and tried their very best to protect and shift the residents. The police succeeded in saving 180 people including women and children. But unfortunately, the lives of late Jafri and 17 others could not be saved.

Sonia Gandhi interjected: 'This is a totally different version from what we were told when we visited Gujarat by your own officers.... (interruptions) There were only two constables posted there—this is what we were told.'

And Somnath Chatterjee said:

> I hope that there would be some record of what has been said there. If that has been recorded, then please look into it. It is a very serious matter, Mr. Home Minister. The Members of Parliament were there. We were given some version and you have been asked to give a different version. We take the strongest exception to this... (interruptions)

Chatterjee said, 'We are not satisfied and therefore we are staging a walk-out,' and he and his party, CPI(M), members left the House, followed by Sonia Gandhi and Congress members at 9:44 PM.

Neither Advani nor others in BJP realized that the Gujarat riots would have a long-term impact on the political fortunes of the party and the coalition government. It was similar to the stupor that Narasimha Rao displayed after the Babri Masjid demolition. Congress party seems to have sensed that this could be a turning point. Congress President Sonia Gandhi, speaking at the Confederation of Indian Industry (CII) annual meeting on 26 April, revealed the change in mood and took the opportunity to raise broader questions about Gujarat and reforms and economic growth.

She started off on a bold note: 'When the Leader of the Opposition is invited by the country's leading industrialists to start off their annual get-together, it is natural to speculate—now what could be the motive; what sort of political winds are blowing and in what direction!'

She highlighted Gujarat's vibrant economy and contrasted it with its social discord. She was no doubt overstating the case like a politician would, but the issue and the questions were pertinent. She said:

> Gujarat has been a model CII state. It is among India's most urbanised and industrialised regions. It is India's most globalised society. In the 1990s, it's economic growth rate was on par with that of the East Asian tigers. It has produced outstanding businessmen and women. But it is a colossal tragedy that growing economic success is being accompanied by social discord. But it is a colossal tragedy that economic globalisation has been accompanied by communal polarisation.

She raised her criticism of Gujarat from a partisan level to that of ideas and ideology, of principles and ethics. It was a good political strategy.

Dramatis Personae

Atal Bihari Vajpayee, a Moderate Right-Wing Nationalist

Atal Bihari Vajpayee had helped BJP to gain general acceptance among Indian political parties. He did it by accepting the modern Indian political inheritance, including the 42nd Constitutional Amendment which introduced the words 'socialist' and 'secular' in the Preamble. He also accepted the Nehruvian legacy without reservations. This was something that BJP could never understand but they let Vajpayee be because they grudgingly trusted his political instincts. He learnt much more from Nehru than any of the Congressmen and Congresswomen, perhaps including his daughter, Indira Gandhi. But he took from Nehru what he wanted and remained what he was, the man on the political right. He was an incendiary speaker who could incite communal passions but he held it on leash, used it occasionally to retain his credentials as a Hindu politician and survived in the Hindu political party that BJS was.

From early on, he cultivated a pan-Indian outlook, something he had inherited from Nehru. At his second speech at the United Nations as India's foreign minister in 1978, Vajpayee ended his speech with a quote from the Tamil Jain poet Thiruvalluvar. The Jana Sangh politicians came to be seen as North Indian and Hindi heartland voices who did not resonate with the rest of the multilingual, multicultural country. Vajpayee went out of his way to project a pan-Indian image for himself. In 1980, when BJP was formed, he was elected the first president, and he tactfully coined the phrase 'Gandhian socialism' to guide the party's programme. It was a bold attempt to deflect the accusation against Hindu right-wing leaders that they were anti-Gandhi. There is no doubt that it was the influence of Jayaprakash Narayan (JP), who was a Gandhian in his own way, on Vajpayee which was reflected in the Hindutva party's new avatar. Vajpayee had always tried to steer the party towards the Centre, and when it lurched towards the extreme right in the late 1980s and early 1990s, he did not voice his dissent but kept a low profile. And he used his rhetorical powers to defend the sins of the extreme rightists in his party. It is this which casts a doubt on his liberal credentials.

It would be a mistake to think of Vajpayee as a liberal in a right-wing party. Although he was a liberal in his personal life, in his politics he remained a regular right-winger, who was firmly anti-communist, which also meant being anti-Soviet Union in the Cold War tussle. What made Vajpayee a true right-winger was that he was an uncompromising nationalist, who believed that India should assert itself wherever and whenever it could and he believed that India's past glory should be fully broadcast. He cannot be labelled a chauvinist or xenophobic as many right-wingers would be, but he was quite attached to the ancient, yes, Hindu peaks of excellence. The attachment to ancient Hindu India did not make him fully hostile to the medieval, Muslim past. But he was certainly not too fond of it in his politics. He had no problems living with it. It is this complexity of his cultural attitudes that made him a better Hindu right-wing politician. He was not intellectually tall and he never made any claims either. In some ways, it was a boon to his politics that he was not weighed down by intellectual baggage, either of Hindutva or of secularism.

The term 'reactionary' should not be seen as an abusive word because its antonym 'rebel' commands a lot of respect and admiration even if the rebellion happens to be an empty gesture. Vajpayee was a political reactionary out of necessity as well as proclivity. He was not a fanatical anti-secularist, and he felt the need to defend the cause of those who were being thrown into the hell of reactionaries by the cavalier secularists. He fully defended the Hindu religious values which were embedded in the Indian civilization. Vajpayee gave political substance to the word 'reactionary'.

He was, however, keenly aware of the present-day challenges such as poverty, illiteracy and disease, and he was pragmatic enough to adopt the most effective methods to combat them. He was pro-reforms because he thought that that would be the best way to deal with the situation. Like Rao, but for different reasons, Vajpayee was not an ardent advocate of economic reforms. Vajpayee played the pragmatist card to pursue reforms to the extent they were pursued. The second-generation reforms never really took off during Vajpayee's prime ministerial tenure.

What is intriguing about Vajpayee's years as prime minister was the fact that he did not leave his personal stamp as much as he should have. Here was a man who was articulate and eloquent, but it always seemed that he was hemmed in by coalition constraints, on the one hand, and the right-wingers in his own party who were not too happy with his soft-pedalling of issues, on the other. As a result, Vajpayee did not find room to express fully and to direct policy as much as he could have. He was forced to manage a delicate balance, and all his energies were used in doing that. But he played the patient head of the family of NDA and kept the flock together. BJP was intent on proving that unlike other non-Congress governments of Janata Party in 1977 and the

National Front in 1989 which did not last the full term, it would run the whole course. Vajpayee was instrumental in holding the government for five years.

In the six years he was prime minister, the NDA government was faced with crises of one kind or other, like the toppling of his government in March 1999, the Kargil episode in May–June 1999, the hijacking of the Indian Airlines plane to Kandahar in December 1999, the terror attack in December 2001, and the Godhra and post-Godhra carnage in Gujarat in February–March 2002. The Lahore trip in February 1999 and the talks with Pakistani President Pervez Musharraf in Agra in July 2001 did not become the successes they could have been. The nuclear test explosions in May 1998 and the claim that India had become a nuclear weapon state were limited successes in the Pakistan context because Islamabad retaliated with its own version of nuclear test explosions. It was, however, a decision that seemed to have altered US perceptions about India and it had also led to strategic talks between the two countries, which paved the way for the civil nuclear deal.

Vajpayee, in many ways, reminds one of the interwar German politician Gustav Stresemann, who steered the difficult years of the Weimar Republic in the 1920s and pitchforked his country back into the comity of nations in Europe by working closely with arch-rival France. Germany, the guilty country of the First World War, was admitted to the League of Nations, which marked the pinnacle of Stresemann's political career. He was awarded the Nobel Peace Prize in 1926. He lasted as chancellor of Germany for a short term of one and a half years, but he was the foreign minister for the rest of the years until he died in 1929 at the age of 51. By temperament and ideology, he was a right-winger. It is said that he would have preferred to serve the Hohenzollerns, the Prussian ruling family-turned-emperors of united Germany in 1871, but the royal family had to go off the political stage at the end of the war in 1918. He shifted his loyalty to the Weimar Republic, which emerged from the ashes of the Hohenzollerns at the end of the war. He did not like the new republican, constitutional set-up for its liberal values but as a symbol of the German nation. Stresemann, a German nationalist at heart, was however clear-headed enough to see that Germany had to learn to live with its European neighbours as among equals. At home, Stresemann was criticized for being soft on Hitler's failed putsch in Munich and for being hard on the communists. Vajpayee was like Stresemann, a narrow-minded nationalist. The phrase 'narrow-minded' need not carry the pejorative connotation that it carries in the talk of the liberals. It could be taken to mean someone who is more comfortable within the confines of one's own nationalism, with no loud declarations of internationalism. In practice, both Stresemann and Vajpayee accepted internationalism in political relations among countries. Vajpayee was wise enough to see reality written large on the wall, and his overtures to Pakistan sprang from this pragmatism. Like Stresemann, Vajpayee was intensely disliked by the right-wingers in his party.

Vajpayee was also like P.V. Narasimha Rao, but without Rao's intellectual interests and pretensions. They were extreme pragma-tists. Vajpayee had the flair to be an inspired leader, but he did not ever exercise it. Rao had never showed any promise of being an inspired leader. In his politics, Vajpayee had a rhetorical fire, which Rao lacked. Vajpayee used this fire to keep the NDA gov-ernment going, but it was not sufficient to win the election in 2004 at the end of his full term as prime minister.

Dramatis Personae

Sonia Gandhi, an Emergent Leader

Congress followed the pattern set in place in the wake of the assassination of Indira Gandhi on 31 October 1984. Rajiv Gandhi, who was away in Calcutta, returned and he was sworn in as prime minister. He was general secretary of the party at the time. Sonia Gandhi did not hold any party office during the time she was with her mother-in-law and prime minister, Indira Gandhi, nor did she take part in any political activity when Rajiv Gandhi was the prime minister. She played the hostess as prime minister's wife, which was ceremonial in nature. She did campaign for Rajiv Gandhi in Amethi in 1984 and 1989 and again in 1991. That was her brush with politics.

When she came back to accept the post of party president in 1998 after six and a half years of seclusion, it was overlooked that she was made president once before which she had turned down. Sitaram Kesri, who replaced Rao as party president, requested Gandhi to campaign for the party. Her first public statement as a Congressperson was in January 1998 in Bangalore and then in Hyderabad. On 15 January, she spoke out in Bangalore:

> The last seven Years have been Years of sorrow and intro-spection for me. Ever since my husband was assassinated, I have chosen to remain a private person. My grief and loss have been deeply personal. But in these years I have also travelled to different parts of India and met people from all walks of life. They have shared our grief and offered my children and me their sympathy and support. For this we will always be grateful.

On 6 April, she was elected party president, and in her remarks as president, she stated the position of Congress:

> I have come to this office at a critical point in the history of Party. Our numbers in Parliament have dwindled. Our support base among the electorate has been seriously eroded. Some segments of our voters—including our tribals, dalits and minorities—have drifted from us. We are in danger of losing our central place in the polity of our country as the natural party of governance.

And she was realistic about her own role: 'I am no saviour, as some of you might want to believe.'

Within a year, however, there was a political crisis, within and outside the party. The BJP-led coalition government fell when AIADMK withdrew support. Gandhi explained at a party meeting of CWC on 6 May that Congress could not form an alternative govern-ment with support from other secular parties in the Opposition.

She squarely blamed SP for working clandestinely with BJP, which prevented Congress from forming a government. She said:

> It is entirely appropriate that the Samajwadi Party has found its destiny in the arms of the communal forces in this country. The clandestine contacts between the leaders of the Samajwadi Party and the BJP have ruthlessly revealed the nexus between them, a nexus which has led to the present situation.

Congress lost the election and its numbers came down to 116, the lowest ever for the party. But this was a few months down the line.

At the CWC meeting on 15 May 1999, Sonia Gandhi resigned from the post of president. She said,

> At this morning's meeting of the Congress Working Committee, certain of my colleagues expressed views to the effect that my having been born elsewhere is a liability to the Congress Party. I am pained by their lack of confidence in my ability to act in the best interests of the Party and the country.

And she announced: 'In these circumstances, my sense of loyalty to the party and my sense of duty to the country compel me to tender my resignation from the post of the Party president.'

Things, however, changed. Sonia Gandhi was back as president on 25 May; she spoke with certain anger, and she indirectly pointed out the issues which were at stake. She said:

> It was in 1998 that I entered the political arena, having consistently refused over the previous seven years to do so. You are well aware of the circumstances which compelled me to take this step.... A year-and-a-half later this is where I am.... The very people who had come to me with folded hands to plead that I emerge from my seclusion to save the Congress began questioning my patriotism.

The colleagues whose names she did not mention were Sharad Pawar, P.A. Sangma and Tariq Anwar. They worked with her for a year.

Although she had harped on the issue of her patriotism, it was not the issue that led to the three members questioning her suitability. Sonia Gandhi came to the point indirectly: 'As regards the post of Prime Minister, as is customary when the occasion arises, this will be decided by the Congress Parliamentary Party.'

The possible inference is that Congress could not form an alternative government because SP did not want to be seen as having placed Sonia Gandhi in the prime minister's post. It would appear that Pawar, Sangma and Anwar felt that this posed a serious problem to the party to form a government based on the support of other parties. They also sensed that there was a general political sentiment which was not in favour of Sonia Gandhi as prime minister. They did not object to her being the president of the party. As a matter of fact, they wanted her to continue to lead the party.

And a little earlier in the speech, she pointed out:

> Our objective is not to win elections alone. In life, there is both success and failure. Victory ultimately goes to those who stand up for truth, who are ready to sacrifice their all for their principles. I want that Congress which is prepared to do this. Let those who wish to go with me do so knowing this full well, and let those with the slightest reservations about this go their own way.

Pawar, Sangma and Anwar went out of the party and formed the Nationalist Congress Party. Sonia Gandhi as president of Congress reached out to Pawar to form an alliance with the new party to fight the Maharashtra assembly elections in November 1999. Five years later, she reached out to Pawar to enter into a coalition to form UPA. Sonia Gandhi, when the time came in 2004, did not accept the office of prime minister, and she nominated Manmohan Singh. Both Sonia Gandhi and Sharad Pawar displayed sagacity and pragmatism, and put aside their differences, which were not personal. Pawar had legitimate political apprehensions about the suitability of Sonia Gandhi as prime minister. Sonia Gandhi did not miss the point, and this was shown in the decision she took in 2004. It also showed that Congress would not function without a member of the Nehru–Gandhi family leading the party.

Sonia Gandhi had also adopted a calibrated stance on the economy, on liberalization and on the need to address the needs of the poor. In her first speech to the party as president on 6 April 1998, she touched upon the prickly issue of economic reforms and there was a strong belief in the party that the election defeat in 1996 was due to economic liberalization programmes carried out by Prime Minister P.V. Narasimha Rao and Finance Minister Manmohan Singh:

> I now draw your attention to a subject which has aroused some controversy. This relates to the programmes of liberalisation and globalisation. We have been told that we have compromised with our basic economic ideology.... It was a path charted out by my husband and carried forward by Shri P.V. Narasimha Rao.

She underlined the fact that there was a connection between reforms, growth and social welfare measures to help the poor. Whoever gave the input to her speech on the issue had put forward a good argument:

> First of all, we need to build a strong resurgent economy which can grow annually at 7–8 per cent. We need this order of growth to create new job opportunities for our expanding labour force and to increase the resource base of our economy so as to devote more resources for poverty alleviation Programmes. Economic reforms—liberalisation and measured opening out to the rest of the world are essential for this purpose.

But she showed a constant awareness of the fears people had developed about economic liberalization. She said: 'I am aware of the doubts and fears about liberalisation and globalisation. It is our duty to dispel them.'

She was clear in her mind about the economic model to be followed when she spoke at the CII annual meeting on 26 April 2002:

> The mixed economy has been an article of faith with us. It has stood the test of time. But I am aware of your doubts on its relevance today. Let me allay your fears. We see a mixed economy as one that integrates effective public investment with vibrant private initiative. We see a mixed economy as one that integrates faster economic growth with deeper social development. We see a mixed economy that integrates increased globalisation with greater self-reliance. A mixed economy is an economy where enterprise is freed from controls but where the government has not lost control. It is that balance the Congress governments (in the states) are trying to achieve.

And she included some hard economic thinking as well: 'We reject irresponsible fiscal management. Our states (state governments) are practicing what we preach. Bankruptcy in public finances is anti-poor.'

XVI

Chapter

SONIA'S REVENGE

In April 2004, Pranab Mukherjee and Kapil Sibal came to brief the media, a few weeks before Lok Sabha election polls. Mukherjee requested the media to carry the Congress point of view. A few days earlier, Sibal pleaded with the media that they should not black out Congress. When a reporter reminded Mukherjee that Mahatma Gandhi appealed to the people directly and did not depend on media, he said that times have changed and that political parties need media to put forward their views and programmes before the people. BJP's senior leader and Deputy Prime Minister L.K. Advani expressed concern that Congress was fading away and that it was not good for Indian democracy. He was of the view that there had to be a credible opposition party. No one expected Congress to lead a coalition government in May. When the results came, and BJP lost, its party president, Venkaiah Naidu, expressed genuine bewilderment. He said that everywhere he went, people spoke highly of Atal Bihari Vajpayee and he confessed that he could not understand why NDA lost. Another BJP leader Arun Jaitley was angry when he was asked in an interview in the run up to the election whether the 'Shining India' campaign would backfire. Even after the results came in, and it was certain that Congress would form the government, the Congress election room people were surprised that the party got 147 seats. They were expecting not more than 130.

BJP leaders became a little accustomed to being in power, and they showed signs of aggression and intolerance that came with office and which was a natural attitude of a right-wing authoritarian party. BJP members of the government were conscious of their own mood and attitude. The media accepted the BJP mood as an inexorable fact. There were no murmurs of protest. The media accepted authoritarian attitude of the ruling party without much ado. Jaswant Singh, who was the finance minister in the outgoing government, was imperious when he faced the media before elections and dismissed the idea that there was any need for course correction in the policy of economic reforms. Advani, who was an ardent critic of economic reforms during 1991–1996, when asked during the election campaign whether he changed his views on liberalization, said, 'How can I say I oppose reforms when I am part of the government which had implemented it?'

The next big moment after the victory was the meeting in the Central Hall of Parliament where the elected Congress members of Parliament met in the early hours of the night of 18 May after Party President Sonia Gandhi had announced that she would not be prime minister. As media reporters watched from the galleries, there was a bit of mess. There were many Congress members who were trying to crowd around Sonia Gandhi. Priya Ranjan Dasmunsi, standing at the lectern, was desperately trying to bring order and quiet. Rahul Gandhi, Priyanka Gandhi Vadra and Robert Vadra also came, and they were sitting in the front row. Many of the Congress members went up to them and pleaded with them to convince their mother. Rahul and Priyanka made it clear that it was for their mother to decide. Many of them were crying and sobbing.

Meanwhile, BJP's women leaders, Sushma Swaraj and Uma Bharati, declared that they would shave off their heads as a mark of protest if Sonia Gandhi became prime minister. The rumour did the rounds in media circles that President A.P.J. Abdul Kalam had cited a law by which Italy would have to create a reciprocal law that would enable an Indian settled in Italy, if elected, to take up a high constitutional office in Rome. Theories of conspiracy, the staple of Delhi's political circles, were choking the Delhi summer air. Many people among Delhi's chattering classes were not only shocked by the poll victory of Congress, but they were also aghast at the prospect of Sonia Gandhi becoming the prime minister of the country.

Sonia Gandhi read out a written statement where she said that she was listening to her inner voice and that it was not her aim to be the prime minister. Manmohan Singh, who was the leader of the party in Rajya Sabha and who functioned as leader of Opposition through the six years from 1998 to 2004, was named prime minister. He was the choice of Sonia Gandhi. It seemed that Congress had crossed the first big post-victory hurdle with dignity and through a superior political tactic. By stepping aside, Sonia Gandhi had defanged her political enemies.

At the first meeting of UPA at 7, Race Course Road, Sonia Gandhi walked into the crowd of waiting media on the lawns and joked that they are not really too long in forming the government and settling issues. Pranab Mukherjee who had taken over as defence minister was all praise for the men in uniform and their punctuality. It was as if the election result had infused a breath of fresh air and the mood was light and relaxed.

Manmohan Singh, in his first address to the country as prime minister on 24 June, showed that the mandate of 2004 was different from that of what he did to salvage the Indian economy from 1991 to 1996. He said, 'Economic reform is not only about freeing private enterprise from the shackles of bureaucratic control. It is also about making the government more effective, efficient and people friendly so it can handle better the many tasks that only Governments can perform.' He was acutely aware of how economic reforms benefited a section of the society and left out the others. He observed, 'While many in our country are benefiting from their integration into the market and the global economy, millions of our citizens are still plagued by illiteracy, disease, want, hunger and malnutrition.'

And he stressed the same issue in his speech at the Council on Foreign Relations in New York on 24 September 2004:

> In a world in which information flows are unfettered, growth processes in which some are seen in benefit while others are excluded are not viable. This is particularly sensitive in a democratic polity in which public dissatisfaction can be quickly converted into electoral defeat. This is indeed the message of the recent elections

in India. They were not, as some have said, a vote against reforms. They were a vote against a process of reform that was seen to be unbalanced, a process which neglected the needs of our rural areas and the agricultural economy.

It is not true that BJP-led NDA was completely oblivious to the existence and needs of the poor. There was continuity in policy decisions between the outgoing BJP-led NDA government and the Congress-led UPA government with regard to the poor. In the 2003 Budget, Finance Minister Jaswant Singh announced:

> Mr Speaker, Sir, I am sure you agree that the disadvantaged must always be the first charge on our exchequer. This is our belief, it is our creed; this is also at the heart of 'integral humanism'. Therefore it has been decided, and I want this to be the first announcement that is made, that the Antyodaya Anna Yojana will be expanded from April 1, 2003 to cover an additional 50 lakh families raising the total coverage to more than a quarter of all BPL families during the year 2003–04. The additional budgetary expenditure on this account will be ₹507 crore.

In July 2004, Congress-led UPA's Finance Minister P. Chidambaram announced:

> I propose to continue, and expand, the Antyodaya Anna Yojana. At present 1.5 crore families are covered. These families are provided with 35 kg of food grains per family per month at a highly subsidised price of ₹2 per kg of wheat and ₹3 per kg for rice. 20.76 lakh tonnes of rice and 17.48 lakh tonnes of wheat were distributed under the Scheme in 2003–04. In the current year, I propose to cover 2 crore families. I expect that the off-take of rice and wheat will increase. Consequently, the Antyodaya Anna Yojana will receive a subsidy of nearly ₹3500 crore. A provision for this level of expenditure has been included in the allocation for food subsidy of ₹25,800 crore.

On 14 November, Manmohan Singh launched the Food for Work programme at Aloor in Andhra Pradesh, which was promised in the Budget in July. This was a precursor to the Mahatma Gandhi National Rural Employment Guarantee Act (MGNREGA), which was promised in Chidambaram's Budget speech.

UPA went about its job of what it saw as the requirements of the mandate by first formulating the National Common Minimum Programme (NCMP), a broad framework of policies and programmes that were worked out between Congress and its partners in UPA and the Left Front parties, which included CPI(M), CPI, the Forward Bloc and the Revolutionary Socialist Party (RSP). The government had adopted it on 28 May, and the National Advisory Council (NAC) was set up, said the Press Information Bureau (PIB) in its press release 'with the Chairperson with the rank of a Cabinet Minister and 20 members to be appointed by the Prime Minister. The Advisory Council will oversee the effective implementation of the NCMP'. Sonia Gandhi was the chairperson, and on 23 June, Manmohan Singh nominated 12 members. The first meeting was held on 17 July, and Sam Pitroda, one of the members, made a presentation. It was decided to present specific result-oriented programmes to be implemented by the ministries. The NAC members later met the prime minister.

On 20 October, PIB press statement said:

> The National Advisory Council has recommended setting up of a National Health Mission aimed at integration of all health programmes and to improve the delivery systems. The NAC at its meeting chaired by Smt. Sonia Gandhi in New Delhi today decided to forward the proposal for the national mission to the Government for early implementation.

And on 12 April 2005, the prime minister launched the National Rural Health Mission.

> I am extremely happy to be here today to launch the National Rural Health Mission. This is truly an important day for our Government and a very special day for me. We are today fulfilling one of the most important promises

of the UPA Government to the people of our country. The slow improvement in the health status of our people has been a matter of great concern. There is no denying the fact that we have not paid adequate attention to this dimension of development thus far. I am, therefore, particularly delighted to launch this new Mission of our Government.

On 2 February 2006, Manmohan Singh launched the flagship programme of UPA, MGNREGA, at Bandlapalli, a village in Andhra Pradesh.

XVII | Chapter

MANMOHAN'S FINEST HOUR

The major event of the UPA's first term in office was the India–US civil nuclear deal, which spread over from July 2005, starting with the joint statement issued in Washington by Manmohan Singh and President George W. Bush to the no-confidence motion against UPA in September 2008. The process had started during the NDA term in office, after the second nuclear test at Pokhran in 1998. In November 2001, it was decided to take the India–US relations to the Next Steps in Strategic Partnerships (NSSP), and this was started in January 2004. Vajpayee, in a statement at the launch of NSSP, mentioned the nuclear technology as one of the areas of cooperation. In his statement on 13 January 2004, Vajpayee said:

> In November 2001, President Bush and I committed our countries to a strategic partnership.... Today we announce the next steps in implementing our shared vision. India and the United States of America agree to expand cooperation in three specific areas: civilian nuclear activities, civilian space programmes, and high technology trade. In addition, we agree to expand our dialogue on missile defence. Cooperation in these areas will deepen the ties of commerce and friendship between our two nations, and will increase stability in Asia and beyond.

In his interaction with the media, his first press conference as prime minister and the first for a prime minister in a decade, Manmohan Singh on 4 September 2004 referred to the strategic relations talks between India and the United States:

> It is my expectation that the agreements relating to the first phase of the Next Steps In Strategic Partnership (NSSP) with the United States would be finalized soon as

the Foreign Secretary is visiting Washington DC in the coming fortnight for final negotiations on this subject. This will enable closer bilateral cooperation in the areas of science and technology and space exploration.

President Bush and Prime Minister Manmohan Singh issued a joint statement in Washington on 19 July 2005, which began the long process that dominated the first term in office of UPA. It became politically contentious because UPA was depending on the Left parties for support.

'Recognizing the significance of civilian nuclear energy for meeting growing global energy demands in a cleaner and more efficient manner', the two leaders discussed India's plans to develop its civilian nuclear energy programme.

President Bush conveyed his appreciation to the prime minister over India's strong commitment to preventing WMD proliferation and stated that as a responsible state with advanced nuclear technology, India should acquire the same benefits and advantages as other such states. The president told the prime minister that he would work to achieve full civil nuclear energy cooperation with India as it realizes its goals of promoting nuclear power and achieving energy security. The president would also seek agreement from Congress to adjust US laws and policies, and the United States would work with friends and allies to adjust international regimes to enable full civil nuclear energy cooperation and trade with India, including but not limited to expeditious consideration of fuel supplies for safeguarded nuclear reactors at Tarapur. In the meantime, the United States would encourage its partners to also consider this request expeditiously. India had expressed its interest in ITER and a willingness to contribute. The United States would consult with its partners considering India's participation. The United States would also consult with the other participants in the Generation IV International Forum with a view towards India's inclusion.

The Prime Minister conveyed that for his part, India would reciprocally agree that it would be ready to assume the same responsibilities and practices and acquire the same benefits and advantages as other leading countries with advanced nuclear technology, such as the United States. These responsibilities and practices consist of identifying and separating civilian and military nuclear facilities and programs in a phased manner and filing a declaration regarding its civilians facilities with the International Atomic Energy Agency (IAEA); taking a decision to place voluntarily its civilian nuclear facilities under IAEA safeguards; signing and adhering to an Additional Protocol with respect to civilian nuclear facilities; continuing India's unilateral moratorium on nuclear testing; working with the United States for the conclusion of a multilateral Fissile Material Cut Off Treaty; refraining from transfer of enrichment and reprocessing technologies to states that do not have them and supporting international efforts to limit their spread; and ensuring that the necessary steps have been taken to secure nuclear materials and technology through comprehensive export control legislation and through harmonization and adherence to Missile Technology Control Regime (MTCR) and Nuclear Suppliers Group (NSG) guidelines.

The issue of civilian nuclear cooperation was quite a complicated one. It seemed that the United States was anxious to get India on board because there was the feeling that it was better to have India, the nuclear weapons state, on their side rather than on the other side. And to do this, the Americans seemed willing to overlook the Pakistan sulk for the favours the United States was showing to its arch-rival in the neighbourhood.

Indian and American negotiators had gone about it with a clear idea. The Americans had recognized that India's strategic—that is, nuclear weapons—programme could not be brought under the American umbrella, though the pressures would continue to be there. So the international safeguards, and the Additional Protocol with the International Atomic Energy Agency (IAEA), would have to be restricted to the civilian nuclear facilities. And it was India that would decide on the division of the nuclear facilities into the civil and military ones. There must have been huge pressures on the Indian negotiators to transfer sophisticated and advanced nuclear facilities open to IAEA safeguards. Manmohan Singh looked beyond. He seemed to have felt, and it was something that strategic experts during the NDA period also believed that India's long-term security interests would be better served by becoming part of the international security architecture, and to work from within the system. It was the same idea that was behind India working through the framework of international economic institutions such as WTO, IMF, WB, and informal groupings like G20 after the 2008 economic recession.

The nuclear scientists in India, on the other hand, especially those who had retired from service, were unhappy and agitated because they felt that decades-long indigenous nuclear developments wrought by the Indians were then being abandoned. BJP was picking its cues from the disenchanted nuclear scientists, arguing that India's long-term strategic interests were being bartered. The Left parties also argued that they were not against nuclear power, but they did not believe that the India–US civil nuclear deal would ensure that. The Left politicians did not want to accept the harsh reality that the United States was an influential player on the international stage, and that without US help India would not be able to reach out to uranium supplies and technology from other countries such as Australia, Japan, Russia and even South Korea.

In his suo motu statement that he made in Parliament on 27 February 2006, Manmohan Singh explained the compulsions to deal with the United States:

> However, international trade in nuclear material, equipment and technologies is largely determined by the Nuclear Suppliers' Group (NSG)—an informal group of 45 countries. Members include the United States, Russia, France and the United Kingdom. India has been kept out of this informal arrangement and therefore denied access to trade in nuclear materials, equipment and various kinds

of technologies. It was with this perspective that we app-
roached negotiations with the United States on enabling
full civilian nuclear energy cooperation with India.

And he gave details of the negotiations being carried out:

> At the official level, we have constituted two groups com-
> prising key functionaries concerned with strategic and
> nuclear matters. They included the Department of Atomic
> Energy, the Ministry of External Affairs, the Armed Forces
> and my Office. These two groups were respectively man-
> dated to draw up an acceptable separation plan, and to
> negotiate on this basis. The directive given to both groups
> was to ensure that our strategic nuclear programme is
> not compromised in any way, while striving to enlarge
> avenues for full civil nuclear energy cooperation with the
> international community. The negotiations by our officials
> have been extensive and prolonged. These have focused
> on four critical elements: the broad contours of a
> Separation Plan; the list of facilities being classified civil-
> ian; the nature of safeguards applied to facilities listed in
> the civilian domain; and the nature and scope of changes
> expected in US domestic laws and NSG guidelines to
> enable full civilian nuclear energy cooperation with India.

He spelled out the difficulties involved in the negotiations:

> At the same time, we are not underestimating the difficul-
> ties that exist in these negotiations. There are complex
> issues involved. Several aspects of the nuclear programme
> lend themselves in the public discussions to differing
> interpretations, such as the Fast Breeder Programme or
> our fuel-cycle capabilities such as re-processing and
> enrichment requirements. The nature and range of strate-
> gic facilities that we consider necessarily outside safe-
> guards constitute yet another example. We have however
> conveyed to our interlocutors that while discussing the
> Separation Plan, there are details of the nature and content
> of our strategic requirements that we cannot share. We will

not permit information of national security significance to be compromised in the process of negotiation.

He also made it clear that Indian nuclear research and developments were not being thrown away. As a matter of fact, he argued that it was because of the achievements of the nuclear scientists that the United States and others had come forward to engage with India. He said:

> We have made it clear that we cannot accept safeguards on our indigenous Fast Breeder Programme. Our scientists are confident that this technology will mature and that the programme will stabilize and become more robust through the creation of additional capability. This will create greater opportunities for international cooperation in this area as well. An important reason why the US and other countries with advanced nuclear technologies are engaging with India as a valued partner is precisely because of the high respect and admiration our scientists enjoy internationally, and the range and quality of the sophisticated nuclear programme they have managed to create under the most difficult odds. This gives us confidence to engage in these negotiations as an equal partner.

On 8 July, the Left withdrew its support to UPA, which had lasted for four years. UPA decided to seek a vote of confidence to prove its majority, though there was no real need to do so. But the confidence motion, which was moved on 21 July, was used to explain the advantages of the India–US civil nuclear deal and show the critics to be wrong. Manmohan Singh stood his ground and the Congress party stood with him on the India–US civilian nuclear deal.

One who rose to the bait was Leader of Opposition, L.K. Advani. He said:

> Mr. Prime Minister, sometimes, I feel that the Deal is not a deal between two sovereign countries; it seems to be a kind of an agreement between two individuals and if one of the individuals happens to be the Prime Minister of our

country, he thinks that nothing else is more important than to fulfil this engagement.

He said that he was not against nuclear energy, nor against closer strategic ties with America, but to its unequal nature where India remained a junior partner. And he made clear the intention of BJP and NDA:

> We have all along maintained that if the people of the country vote NDA again to power, we will renegotiate this deal. We haven't said that we will scrap it. We have said that we will renegotiate this deal to make it a Treaty between equals so that there are no constraints on our strategic options and no constraint on our strategic autonomy.

The Left Front and Congress argued closely about the UPA–Left coordination committee that was set to oversee the negotiations over the deal. The Left Front said that it withdrew support because the protocol of the coordination committee was not honoured. The government did not share the text of the agreement between India and IAEA with the committee. The government offered two answers. The first was that this was a confidential document and the government could just share the substance of the agreement. The second was that the Left Front did not show enough patience and did not take into account the time zone differences between New Delhi and Geneva, which is the headquarters of IAEA. The case was closely argued by External Affairs Minister Pranab Mukherjee, Finance Minister P. Chidambaram and CPI(M)'s Basudeb Acharia. The argument over the coordination committee was a Rashomon process, where three different narratives were given of the same event.

Pranab Mukherjee explained what the coordination committee was all about:

> The mandate of the committee was to address the concerns of the Left Parties on the impact of the Hyde Act, impact of the 123 Agreement, and the impact on both India's independent foreign policy and our three-stage

civil nuclear programme, which we had accepted long ago. These concerns of the Left parties will be addressed by this committee, will be taken into account before the operationalization of the civil nuclear cooperation. Please remember these are the words we used. The text was drafted by myself and one of the important Left leaders. As he is a member of the other House, I am not mentioning his name. The operative part was that after we finalise the findings of the committee, the findings of the committee would be submitted to the chairperson of the UPA. It is because this mechanism was established by the UPA chairperson. Sir, it was not a parliamentary committee appointed by you, it was not a Government committee appointed by the Prime Minister.

P. Chidambaram spoke about the meetings of the UPA–Left coordination committee:

The UPA-Left Committee held nine meetings between Sept 11, 2007 and June 6, 2008. At the fourth meeting on October 9, 2007, the CPI (M)'s members noted that the Left parties were not opposed to a safeguards agreement on principle just as they have not been opposed to the separation plan.

Their objection continued to be to the 123 Agreement. This issue was discussed at the fifth meeting on October 22, 2007 and at the sixth meeting on November 16, 2007. At the sixth meeting, after the exchanges, it was decided that the impact of the provisions of the Hyde Act and the 123 Agreement on the IAEA Safeguards Agreement would have to be examined, and since it required talks with the IAEA Secretariat for working out the text of an India-Specific Safeguards Agreement, the Government will proceed with the talks and the outcome will be presented to the Committee. That is precisely what this Government has done.

It went to the IAEA Secretariat for talks. It froze that text. We came back to Committee on March 17, May 6 and

June 25, and we have reported the outcome of the talks to the committee. We have done nothing in a non-transparent manner.

Then followed Basudeb Acharia's viewpoint:

A joint committee was formed. What was the outcome of the joint committee? The resolution which was adopted in the first meeting of the Left–UPA joint committee was that the operationalization of the deal would depend on the outcome of the findings of this committee.

Acharia argued:

How could the committee come to any conclusion? On 16th of November there was a written understanding that the Government wanted to go to the IAEA to start negotiations and it was assured that the Government would proceed only after the text of the Agreement is placed before the committee and if the committee agrees, then only the Government would go to the IAEA and the NSG. When the committee met in June, the Agreement was not shown to the committee. Without showing the text of the Agreement, how can the committee come to any conclusion? The committee was told that it was a classified document. The same day, from the IAEA, it was stated that there was no restriction and the Government can circulate this text.

Acharia explained what forced the Left parties to withdraw support: 'On 8th July, in a Press Conference, the hon. External Affairs Minister stated that the Government would not go to IAEA before it takes the vote of confidence. The day he made the statement, the Prime Minister announced and the Government went to IAEA.'

The most scathing and succinct criticism of the nuclear deal came from BJP's Maneka Gandhi. She said:

And finally to have come to this pass on such a strange triviality as a deal that will never be signed and never be honoured and has no meaning for India nor does it bring any benefits to anyone in it is perhaps typical of all the other things that the government found important in the last four years.

Manmohan Singh did not seem much worried about the reaction of the Left parties. In reply to the confidence motion, on 22 July, Singh, in a very uncharacteristic manner, hit out against Advani in stringent words:

> As for Shri Advani's various charges, I do not wish to waste the time of the House in rebutting them. All I can say is that before leveling charges of incompetence on others, Shri Advani should do some introspection. Can our nation forgive a Home Minister who slept when the terrorists were knocking at the doors of our Parliament? Can our nation forgive a person who single-handedly provided the inspiration for the destruction of the Babri Masjid with all the terrible consequences that followed? To atone for his sins, he suddenly decided to visit Pakistan and there he discovered new virtues in Mr. Jinnah. Alas, his own party and his mentors in the RSS disowned him on this issue. Can our nation approve the conduct of a Home Minister who was sleeping while Gujarat was burning leading to the loss of thousands of innocent lives? Our friends in the Left Front should ponder over the company they are forced to keep because of miscalculations by their General Secretary.

The reference was to Prakash Karat, the CPI(M) general secretary.

The government won the motion of confidence with 275 Ayes as against 256 Noes.

In the 2009 Lok Sabha election, Advani was the prime ministerial candidate of NDA, and, surprisingly, Manmohan Singh was the prime ministerial candidate for Congress and UPA. Congress and UPA won the election, and Congress improved its tally from 147 to 206.

XVIII Chapter

SPECTRE OF CORRUPTION

The second term of UPA was mired in controversy and charges of corruption. There were allegations that there was major financial misappropriation in connection with the Commonwealth Games in October 2010. But it was the 2G spectrum allocation of January 2008 that ballooned into the biggest scandal for the UPA government. The Opposition, which was looking for ways to find chinks in UPA, latched on to the issue with passion and vigour.

What made the 2G spectrum allocation the big-bang scandal was the release into the public domain of recorded conversations intercepted by the Central Bureau of Investigation (CBI), which revealed influential industrialists, politicians and journalists talking and plotting as to who should be the telecom minister. Then in November 2010, the Comptroller and Auditor General presented its performance audit on the issue of 2G spectrum allocation. Many of Congress politicians attacked CAG Vinod Rai for pursuing a hidden agenda and the criticism seemed indecorous and impolitic. The CAG maintained a dignified silence even as the Opposition parties tried to make the most of the mistakes that the ministry had committed in the process of allocating 2G spectrum. What is of great interest is the explanation offered in the executive summary of the report as to why the audit of the 2G spectrum allocation was taken up in the first place:

> II Why did we decide to do an audit on the Issue of License and allocation of Spectrum now?

> In January 2008, Department of Telecommunications issues 120 new licenses for unified access services on the same day. These issues were issued at price which has been discovered in 2001. Issuance of 120 licenses in just

one day and at a price discovered in 2001 has drawn the attention of Media, Parliament and informed members of the civil society. Questions have been raised regarding the transparency in the allocation process and the failure in the maximization of revenue generation from the allocation of spectrum which is a national asset. This department has been receiving innumerable references from Members of Parliament and other sources repeatedly, questioning the allocation process and the price fixed for such allocation. The claim in each such reference is that ineligible applicants seem to have been granted licences and at a price which appeared far below what has been perceived to be the appropriate market price in 2008.

It does seem strange that the CAG should set out to carry out a performance audit because the issue has been raised in the public domain. The CAG is expected to pinpoint violations of rules and procedures, lapses and indiscretions in the course of its regular audit. The CAG is seen as the financial watchdog of the government, and it is described as the friend, guide and philosopher of the most important parliamentary panel, the Public Accounts Committee (PAC), but it is interesting and surprising that the CAG chose to turn proactive. And that is what it did.

The CAG proffered a weak justificatory argument:

> It was in this context that this department felt that there was a sufficient justification to review the entire process of issuance of licences, award of spectrum and the implementation of the UAS regime. The need for doing so was further justified as six years have passed since the introduction of the UAS regime in 2003. While accepting the Government's prerogative to formulate the policy of UASL it was felt that an in-depth examination of implementation of such policy needed to be done.

The CAG was indeed aggressive, if not hostile, in its approach to the issue. It cited two earlier audits done on telecom as precedents for its exercise on 2G spectrum allocation. The two earlier audits were: 'Package of Concessions Given to Cellular Mobile Operators' presented to Parliament in 2000 and 'Revenue Management in the Department of Telecommunications' undertaken in 2004–2005 and presented to Parliament in May 2006.

According to the CAG, the first main lapse was that the Department of Telecommunications (DoT) had kept the Ministry of Finance out of the process of determining the efficient allocation of spectrum and the right price, and that the DoT did not hold consultations with the Group of Ministers about the pricing of spectrum, instead concentrating on the vacation of spectrum by the military. Second, going against the recommendation of the Telecom Regulatory Authority of India (TRAI) that there should not be any limit on the licenses to be issued, the DoT had issued a press release in September 2007 that the last date would be 1 October 2007, and later changed it to 25 September 2010, further restricting the number of applicants. The third major lapse was that it did not follow the First Come First Served policy because it did not give the 15 days mandatory time for those who were issued letters of intent (LoIs) on a single day, 10 January 2008, which required the submission of performance bank guarantee (PBG) and financial bank guarantee (FBG). There is the wry observation that 'some licensees, who could proactively anticipate such procedural changes were ready with Demand Drafts on dates prior to the notification of cut-off date by DoT and could avail the benefit of first right to allocation of spectrum, having jumped the queue.' The fourth major lapse was:

> Eighty five out of the 122 licences issued in 2008 were found to be issued to Companies which did not satisfy the eligibility conditions set by the DoT and had suppressed facts, disclosed incomplete information and submitted fictitious documents for getting UAS licences and thereby access to spectrum.

The next major finding of the CAG was with regard to the much-debated presumptive loss. The report noted under the heading 'Presumptive Value of Spectrum Allocated to 122 New UAS Licencees and 35 Dual Technology Licencees in 2007–08':

▌ Any loss ascertained while attempting to value the 2G spectrum allocated to 122 licensees can only be 'presumptive', given the fact that there varied determinants like its scarcity value, the nature of competition, business plans envisaged, number of operators, growth of sector etc. which, depending upon the market situation would throw up the price that commands at a given point of time.

The important and interesting point was about what is meant by presumptive value and loss:

▌ Instead of attempting to come to a specific value of 2G spectrum which could have been only possible only through an efficient market discovery process, we have looked at the various indicators to assess a possible (presumptive) value, from the records made available to Audit rather than going for any mathematical/econometric models.

The report noted that on 5 November 2007, S Tel Limited wrote to the prime minister offering to pay a higher price than it had applied for the UAS licenses in July/September 2007, 'in the shape of additional revenue share for next ten years. The offer was enhanced by the firm with a stipulation to further revise it upwards in case of any counter bid'. The CAG working from the amount offered by S Tel Limited had calculated that the 'value of 122 licenses and 35 Dual Technology licenses after discounting for the receivables in future years works out to ₹65,909 crore as against ₹12,386 actually received.'

The next possible/presumptive value/loss of 2G spectrum was based on the comparative price of auctioned 3G spectrum. The TRAI had recommended in its report submitted to the government in September 2006 that 3G spectrum should be auctioned. And in its 2010 report, it said that 3G prices should be adopted for 2G in the 1,800 MHz band.

▌ If these recommendations, which have not so far been accepted by the Government are taken into account, then the value of 2G spectrum allotted to 122 licencees and 35 Dual Technology licencees would be much higher at about ₹1,52,038 crores as against the amount actually received.

The third possible/presumptive value loss was based on FDI that those companies which obtained the licenses were able to generate. The CAG said, the 'Value of a new company with no experience in the Telecom sector can primarily be taken as that of the licence and access to spectrum.' Based on this calculation, the value of the allocated 2G spectrum to the 122 licensees and the 35 dual technology licensees would be between '₹7,758 crore and ₹9,100 crore as against ₹1,658 crore priced by DoT' for a pan-Indian license. Similarly, the total value of spectrum allocated to the 122 licensees and 35 dual technology licensees 'would be between ₹58,000 to ₹68,000 crores as against the actual revenue of ₹12,386 crores realised'.

The Opposition parties latched on to the CAG report and demanded the setting up of a JPC. The government resisted the demand, and the reasoning was that PAC, the most important parliamentary committee, would be scrutinizing the 2G spectrum allocation based on the CAG report and that CBI was already investigating the issue of licenses and that the Supreme Court was monitoring the enquiry. The Opposition parties argued that either Prime Minister Manmohan Singh was in the know of the blatant violation of procedures that Telecom Minister A. Raja had committed in doling out favours, or if he did not know, then Singh was guilty of presiding over a cabinet over which he did not have much control. Raja belonged to DMK, a member of the ruling coalition, UPA, then Singh was guilty of presiding over a cabinet over which he did not have much control.

The government agreed to the setting up of the JPC during the Budget session of 2011. And Singh made his first public defence about the 2G spectrum allocation in his reply to the Motion of Thanks to the Address of the President in the Lok Sabha and in the Rajya Sabha on 24 February 2011. In the Lok Sabha, he said that the telecom policy was sound and it had proved beneficial because it spurred increase in teledensity in the country. Then he cited the statistics. He said that in March 2004, the teledensity in rural areas stood at 1.55 per cent; in urban areas, it was 20.79; and the figure for the country was 7.02 per cent. And then he cited the figures for December 2010: rural areas (31.18%), urban areas (147.8%) and the whole country (66%). He said,

> It turned out to be that while the policy was sound, the way it was implemented, I think, gave rise to problems. Those problems will now be looked into by the JPC; they are being looked into by the PAC; and if there are any criminal aspects they are being looked into by the CBI.

In his reply to the Motion of Thanks to the Address of the President in the Rajya Sabha on the same day (24 February 2011), Singh acknowledged the public furore over the 2G spectrum allocation issue. He said: 'The 2G issue has occupied the front pages of our newspapers for the last several months following the submission of the CAG report.'

The PAC headed by Murli Manohar Joshi, a senior member of BJP, wanted to finalize a report, which was to be an indictment of the prime minister. The Congress members of the PAC did not want that to happen and refused to approve the draft. Joshi went ahead and forwarded the report to Lok Sabha Speaker Meira Kumar. The speaker did not accept the report because it was not approved by the committee. In January 2012, the Supreme Court cancelled the 122 licenses issued on a single day in January 2008. The JPC had not been able to finalize the report because of differences between the Opposition members and the chairman of the committee, P.C. Chacko of Congress.

In April 2011, there came on the scene an anti-corruption activist from Maharashtra, Anna Hazare, who spearheaded a movement for legislating a Lokpal Bill, the Ombudsman Bill, which would check into corruption cases in high places in government. Hazare had undertaken a fast at Delhi's Jantar Mantar on 6 April. On 4 April, the Prime Minister's Office issued a press statement saying that Manmohan Singh met Hazare and his associates on 11 March for more than an hour. The civil society activists presented a draft of the Lokpal Bill. The prime minister had suggested that a sub-committee of a Group of Ministers could meet with them and discuss the draft. The press release said: 'The Sub-Committee headed by Shri A.K. Antony met Shri Hazare's colleagues but the interaction proved fruitless as the activists were insisting on the Government accepting their draft in full.'

The upsurge of popular sentiment forced the government on the back foot, and the prime minister had to form a new committee comprising five cabinet ministers and five civil society activists, including Hazare. They met for a month from 16 May to 16 June. There was a report which was to serve as a basis for the Lokpal Bill. Hazare went on a fast once again on 16 August, and he called it off when he was assured that it would be introduced in Parliament. The Bill was introduced and sent to the Parliamentary Standing Committee during the monsoon session. The Standing Committee came back with its report in November 2011. The Lokpal Bill was introduced and passed in the Lok Sabha on 23 December 2011, but it could not go through the Rajya Sabha, though the Upper House sat late into the night on 29 December 2011. In the Budget session of 2012, the Bill that got struck in the Rajya Sabha was sent to a House Select Committee. The House Select Committee came back with its report, but the Bill was yet to be taken for consideration and passing in the Rajya Sabha. It would then have to go back to the Lok Sabha in its amended form and passed by the Lower House once again.

There was further trouble in 2012 for Manmohan Singh when the CAG observed violations of norms and rules in the allocation of coal blocks to private players between 2006 and 2009 when Singh was the coal minister. The Opposition seized the oppor-tunity to point a finger at the prime minister and even demanded his resignation—which was a mere political gesture, no doubt—because the violations had happened in the ministry which he was heading, and therefore he should own up moral responsibility and quit.

The CAG once again gave reasons for its performance audit:

▌ The widening gap between the demand and domestic
production of coal and consequent import in coal imports
to fill up the gap warranted a study to examine the
adequacy and effectiveness of the action taken by Coal
India Limited (CIL) and the Ministry of Coal (MOC) for
augmentation of coal production.

The performance audit was on 'Allocation of Coal Blocks and Augmentation of Coal Production'.

The CAG noted that a meeting was held with the stakeholders on 28 June 2004 to decide on competitive bidding, and a note on 'competitive bidding for allocation of coal blocks' was submitted on 16 July 2004 to the minister of state, coal and mines, and it was 'highlighted' in it that 'since there is a substantial difference between price of coal supplied by Coal India and coal produced through captive mining, there is a windfall gain to the person who is allotted a captive block.' It was even observed in the note that the 'the bidding system will only tap part of the windfall profit for the public purposes.' It is interesting that the note which went before the minister of state stated rather clearly that there was an inherent windfall gain and a bidding system tapped only part of this windfall gain for public purposes. The CAG observed: 'Despite these facts, the GOI (Government of India) is yet (February 2012) to finalise the modus operandi of competitive bidding.'

The CAG then reached its conclusion based on the evidence that the allocation was not made through competitive bidding in a transparent manner and the windfall profit accrued to the private allottees:

▌ Delay in the introduction of competitive bidding has
rendered the existing process beneficial to the private
companies. Audit has estimated financial gains to the
tune of ₹1.86 lakh crore likely to accrue to private coal
block allottees (based on average cost of production and
average sale price of Opencast mines of CIL in the year

2010–11). A part of this financial gain could have accrued to the national exchequer by operationalising the decision taken years earlier to introduce competitive bidding for allocation of coal blocks. Therefore, audit is of strong opinion that there is a need for strict regulatory and monitoring mechanism to ensure the benefit of cheaper coal is passed on to the consumer.

This provided enough ammunition to the Opposition parties to corner the government and the prime minister who was holding the coal portfolio during that period. The CAG report was quite meticulous and even reticent in pointing out the lacunae in policy, but the politicians had taken the cautious conclusions to be exact facts. BJP's Hansraj Ahir and Prakash Javadekar, complained to the Chief Vigilance Commissioner (CVC), and the CVC found enough substance in the complaint to forward it to the CBI. Meanwhile, the CBI was already probing some of the allocations. In response to a public interest litigation (PIL) plea, the Supreme Court had begun to monitor the CBI probe into the coal block allocations.

At the end of 2012, the UPA government in its eighth year in office found itself covered completely under the cloud of corruption.

Dramatis Personae

Manmohan Singh, the Unquiet Liberal

With Manmohan Singh, the relationship with the United States was more than the civilian nuclear deal and more than the strategic relationship. And in his remark at the National Press Club in Washington on 21 July 2005, he gave a clear hint as to why he valued the American connection. He observed:

> Everywhere I went, right from the President to the Houses of Congress and now to this most prestigious institution that the National Press Club is, I have received and I felt that I am in the company of very intimate friends.

And I know that's a tribute not to me personally but to the country that I represent, an India that is now trying to seek its social and economic salvation in the framework of an open society and an open polity.

The three key words are 'economic salvation', 'open society' and 'open polity'. He could be dismissed as a starry-eyed admirer of the United States, not very different from the young men and women in many parts of Asia and Africa, even Europe.

This fierce passion for an open society flashed again during his opening remarks with some of the newspaper editors he had met at the height of Anna Hazare and Ramdev protests on 29 June 2011:

> Tax evasion is one important source of generation of black money. But there are other issues—narcotics, trafficking in human beings—all these illegal activities.... We need a strong mechanism to track down these criminal elements. But in all these my worry is to avoid a situation when we convert this vast country of over 1.2 billion people into a state where everybody is policing everybody else. We must not bring back the license permit raj which we sought to abolish in 1991.

The more interesting defence that Manmohan Singh had put forward was an anecdote from his student days at Cambridge University earlier in his interaction with the editors:

> When I was a student at Cambridge, Sir Paul Chambers, who was then the Chairman of Imperial Chemical Industries, came and addressed us on who is a good manager, who will be considered by industry as a good manager.

> He told our student group that, in an uncertain world in which we live in, if 5 out of 10 decisions that I take ex-ante turn out to be correct ex-post that would be considered as a job well done. If out of 10 decisions that I take, 7 turn out to be right ex-post that would be considered an excellent performance. But if you have a system which is

required to perform 10 out of 10 cases I think no system can be effective and satisfy that onerous condition.

He was, of course, pleading an impossible case. In the political arena, the mistakes count more than successes, and in his second term as prime minister, the message went out that things were not working well. And at the same time, the economy nosedived.

Manmohan Singh had an advantage that Narasimha Rao and Atal Bihari Vajpayee did not have. The other two prime ministers had to do their own political management, while Congress President Sonia Gandhi did that for Singh. But that did not make any easy the making of difficult decisions for Singh. He was keen to push as much reforms as he could.

Manmohan Singh was also willing to stick his neck out in a way that very few would have dared to do, especially about the benign aspect of British colonialism. He had the intellectual confidence to dare the brickbats. In a speech at the conferment of an honorary doctorate at Oxford University, the Indian prime minister said clearly if not loudly:

> Today, with the balance and perspective offered by the passage of time and the benefit of hindsight, it is possible for an Indian Prime Minister to assert that India's experience with Britain had its beneficial consequences too. Our notions of the rule of law, of a Constitutional government, of a free press, of a professional civil service, of modern universities and research laboratories have all been fashioned in the crucible where an age old civilisation met the dominant Empire of the day. These are all elements which we still value and cherish. Our judiciary, our legal system, our bureaucracy and our police are all great institutions, derived from British–Indian administration and they have served the country well.

> The idea of India as enshrined in our Constitution, with its emphasis on the principles of secularism, democracy, the rule of law and, above all, the equality of all human beings

irrespective of caste, community, language or ethnicity, has deep roots in India's ancient civilisation. However, it is undeniable that the founding fathers of our republic were also greatly influenced by the ideas associated with the age of enlightenment in Europe. Our Constitution remains a testimony to the enduring interplay between what is essentially Indian and what is very British in our intellectual heritage.

Singh did not give up his thinking, and he did not abandon his own worldview even when he knew that they did not count for much, and that is an admirable thing. It is not necessary for anyone to agree with him, but it is important that he had a perspective of his own. He could see clearly certain things about India and Indians which many would not see, or refuse to see. In the Oxford lecture, he was candid enough to observe:

> The economics we learnt at Oxford in the 1950s was also marked by optimism about the economic prospects for the post-War and post-colonial world. But in the 1960s and 1970s, much of the focus of development economics shifted to concerns about the limits to growth. There was considerable doubt about the benefits of international trade for developing countries. I must confess that when I returned home to India, I was struck by the deep distrust of the world displayed by many of my countrymen. We were influenced by the legacy of our immediate past. Not just by the perceived negative consequences of British imperial rule, but also by the sense that we were left out in the cold by the Cold War.

That was a sharp observation to make anytime anywhere.

Manmohan Singh had asserted in a very unassertive way that there was an umbilical cultural and intellectual link between India and the West, and that is what served as the basis for economic liberalization and globalization. He was, however, alert enough to sense the problems when they cropped up. That is why, in his address to the United Nations General Assembly on

24 September 2011, he said: 'Till a few years ago the world had taken for granted the benefits of globalisation and global interdependence. Today we are being called upon to cope with the negative dimensions of those very phenomena.'

He did not, of course, offer a fuller critique, but he knew that there was a problem and that it would not be possible to be starry-eyed about economic liberalization.

THE SHORT LONG MARCH

In the run-up to the 2014 Lok Sabha election, BJP had to make a crucial break with its past. The party since its inception in 1980 was dominated by Atal Bihari Vajpayee and L.K. Advani, and Murli Manohar Joshi was let in for reasons other than Joshi's charisma. It was Vajpayee and Advani who chaperoned the next generation of leaders when they picked them for being president of the party or occupying other key positions. They made Bangaru Laxman president of the party at the Nagpur session in 2000, and when he had to exit because of the tehelka.com sting operation showing him accepting a bribe from an ostensible defence dealer, it was M. Venkaiah Naidu who was chosen to lead the party. But the Vajpayee–Advani duumvirate had to end after the 2004 defeat with Vajpayee as the prime ministerial candidate and after the 2009 defeat when Advani was the party's prime ministerial aspirant. Joshi was never deemed to be in the race for the prime minister's post. The party had to choose from the next-generation leaders, comprising Arun Jaitley and Sushma Swaraj, who were leaders of Opposition in the Rajya Sabha and Lok Sabha respectively. Many BJP chief ministers in the states, such as Shivraj Singh Chouhan in Madhya Pradesh and Raman Singh in Chhattisgarh, were never in the reckoning. The one man who showed clear signs of ambition to be the prime minister was Narendra Modi, the chief minister in Gujarat. He cultivated the image of a BJP leader who was not just a chief minister but also a leader who could speak to the country, and he certainly captivated the party workers across the country. He exuded energy and confidence through aggressive posturing. From 2012 onwards, he was pitching himself as a national leader in the party and no one else even tried to compete with him.

Modi's peers in BJP were not willing to concede readily the edge Modi had developed over them. There were only a few like Arun Jaitley who betted on Modi from early on. Jaitley interpreted the enthusiasm of the party workers for Modi as a kind of democratic approval. He argued that if there were primaries as in the Democratic and Republican parties in the United States, where the party members voted for their candidate, then Modi would win easily. He thought that the workers cheering for Modi was a clear indication that he should be the prime ministerial candidate. The others seemed to have come around to the same view gradually and perhaps reluctantly. No one of them had dared to throw their hat in the prime ministerial ring which Modi was willing to do. In this, he was bold and candid.

BJP, like Congress, does not have a transparent inner-party democratic process in choosing its leaders. The party president and other functionaries are handpicked by the top leaders. Modi had to win over the top leaders. One man who seemed to have been reluctant to endorse Modi as the prime ministerial candidate was Advani, though it was Advani who had groomed Modi; it was Advani who sent him from Delhi to Gujarat to be the chief minister at the end of 2001 to tide over dissensions in the Gujarat unit of the party over then Chief Minister Keshubhai Patel; and it was Advani who backed him to the hilt in Parliament and in the party after the post-Godhra anti-Muslim riots in Gujarat in early March 2002. The reasons for Advani's opposition to his own acolyte were not clear. What was clear was his irritation and unhappiness. He did not attend the National Executive meeting at Panaji in Goa on 8 and 9 June, where it became clear that the younger members of the party were rooting for Modi and they were only too willing to boot out the older lot, including Advani. Party President Rajnath Singh was clearly under pressure to announce the name of Modi. But as party president, he had to display both restraint and propriety. When Advani sent in his resignation from the National Executive and all other decision-making bodies of which he had been a member since the party was founded, Singh had to respond with care.

The Central Parliamentary Board (CPB) passed a resolution on 10 June 2013. It said:

> The BJP Parliamentary Board yesterday decided not to accept Shri L.K. Advani's resignation from the three main fora of the Party—The National Executive, Parliamentary Board and Election Committee and requested him to continue to be a member of these three bodies.

> On behalf of the Party, Shri Rajnath Singh assured Shri Advani that his concerns about the functioning of the Party would be properly addressed and the President will discuss the modalities of addressing these concerns with Shri Advani.

> Today afternoon, RSS Sarsanghchalak, Shri Mohan Bhagwat spoke to Shri Advani and asked him to respect the BJP Parliamentary Board decision and continue to guide the Party in national interest. Shri Advani had decided to accept Shri Bhagwat's advice.

At the end of the two-day National Executive meeting, Singh named Modi as the chairman of the campaign committee for the 2014 Lok Sabha election. The announcement was wildly cheered by the party workers. It seemed clear that this announcement was an unofficial declaration that Modi would be the prime ministerial candidate. Jaitley, praising Singh's decision, said at a conference of party workers outside Panaji after the National Executive meeting that the sign of a good leader is to take the right decisions, and he said that Singh like a good leader had taken the right decision in naming Modi as the campaign committee chairman.

Jaitley and Naidu vigorously supported Modi in their public statements, clearly indicating that Modi was the party's prime ministerial candidate. On 20 June 2013, Naidu's reaction at a press conference at Hyderabad was released by BJP. It said,

> Mr. M. Venkaiah Naidu, a senior leader of the BJP, reacting to the Prime Minister's (Manmohan Singh) comment that 'people know what Modi stands for' said at a Press

Conference in Hyderabad that Narendra Modi, a very popular leader, stands for 3 Ds–Decisive, Dynamic, and Development-oriented. These three Ds are making the most popular leader among the people in the country. Mr Naidu said all these three Ds are missing in the Prime Minister and his government. People want a decisive, dynamic and development-oriented leader and party. That is why they are looking towards the BJP and talking about Narendra Modi.

Jaitley wrote in his blog on 8 July 2013 under the heading 'On Road to 2014':

> While disillusioned with the Congress, the charge against the BJP was that it had not been able to put its own house in order. Its galaxy of leaders was regarded as a liability rather than an asset. Fortunately, the party has now started putting its house in order. The possibility of the party contesting under one leader is real.

On 22 July, Jaitley again wrote a strong defence of Modi with the presumption that Modi was the prime ministerial candidate much ahead of the official announcement on 13 September. Under the heading, 'Why Is the Congress Party Trying to Communalise the 2014 Elections?' he wrote that Congress had always tried to single out Modi for attack and that it had only proved counter-productive. He said,

> The last few weeks have witnessed a crude attempt by the UPA leaders at this strategy. There are three visible indicators of this. Firstly, the UPA has concentrated its attack on Narendra Modi. In Gujarat, the initial strategy of the Congress was to excessively attack Modi. Modi always excelled in this political battle with Congress. He got the better of them. Finding this strategy counter-productive, the Congress then would go back to the alternative strategy of pretending that Modi did not exist as far as their campaign was concerned. At the Centre the Congress strategy in the first phase comprised excessively attacking

Modi. In the process they are conceding the centrestage to him. Soon they will realise the counterproductivity of their strategy and move back to the alternative practice of pretending to ignore Modi.

It was on 13 September 2013, at the end of the CPB meeting, that Party President Rajnath Singh announced that Narendra Modi was the party's prime ministerial candidate. Members of CPB were present at the crowded press conference when Singh made the announcement in Hindi and read out the formal statement in English naming Modi. Modi did not address the press conference. No other leader spoke. They confined themselves to garlanding Modi and congratulating him. While leaving the press, Singh announced that Modi would be calling on Advani at the senior leader's home to seek his blessing.

Modi continued to be the chief minister of Gujarat even as he campaigned vigorously and continuously for the Lok Sabha election. It became clear that Uttar Pradesh was an important part of his poll strategy. He had got his Gujarat party colleague Amit Shah to be in charge of the UP campaign, and it seemed that Singh did not have much say in the matter. Second, even as there was speculation in the media that whether he would want to contest from Lucknow following Atal Bihari Vajpayee, he chose Varanasi as his constituency. It seemed a significant choice because he had chosen a city which was a symbol and centre of Hindu religion and religiosity. He also chose to contest for the Lok Sabha election from Vadodara.

The 2002 Gujarat riots and Modi's handling of it had remained a burning issue, and BJP leaders were quite uneasy about it, though they tried to brush it aside as no more relevant after a decade and three electoral victories of Modi in the state assembly elections. They also argued that there was no legal case against Modi. But it was clear that it was lurking at the back of the minds of both Modi and other BJP leaders. The Opposition too used it as the main issue to oppose Modi. So, when the magistrate's court in Ahmedabad on 26 December 2013 closed the case after the Supreme Court-appointed Special Investigation Team (SIT) on the petition of Zakia Jafri, wife of Ehsan Jafri, a Congress legislator, about the conspiracy in the killing of her husband during the riots at the Gulbarg Housing Society in Ahmedabad the party and Modi felt a sense of relief.

On the same day, Jaitley wrote his blog on the closure of the case, titled 'The Conspiracy of Falsehoods Stands Exposed'. He once again defended Modi and the Gujarat government in their handling of the riots. He said,

> The total number of persons arrested both for preventive and punitive actions are 1,00,488. This is more than the number of persons arrested in any other caste or religious tension in India. More people died in police firing during disturbances than in any other riot. This negates the allegation of police connivance. 4272 cases were registered. 1168 of these cases have been decided and hundreds of accused have been convicted. Most of these actions have been taken by the Gujarat Police.

Modi wrote his blog on 27 December, baring his thoughts about 2002, which he did not do until then. The blog, titled 'Satyameva Jayate: Truth Alone Triumphs', was confessional in nature, and it also had rhetorical flourishes. He wrote: 'The end brings back the memories of the beginning.' And he said: 'This is the first time I am sharing the harrowing ordeal I had gone through in those days at a personal level.' And he described the harrowing ordeal: 'I was shaken to the core. "Grief", "Sadness", "Pain", "Anguish", "Agony"—mere words could not capture the absolute emptiness one felt on witnessing such inhumanity.'

He then stated the defence of his silence, which was seen as sheer brazenness by his critics and opponents: 'During those challenging times, I often recollected the wisdom in our scriptures; explaining those sitting in positions of power did not have the right to share their own pain and anguish. They had to suffer it in solitude.' And he gave a personalized melodramatic turn to the issue:

> However, as if all the suffering was not enough, I was also accused of the death and misery of my own loved ones,

my Gujarati brothers and sisters. Can you imagine the inner turmoil and shock of being blamed for the very events that shattered you! For so many years, they incessantly kept their attack, leaving no stone unturned. What pained even more was that in their overzealousness to hit at me for their narrow political and personal ends, they ended up maligning my entire state and country.

He observed: 'Yesterday's judgment culminated a process of unprecedented scrutiny closely monitored by the highest court of the land, the Honourable Supreme Court of India. Gujarat's trial by fire of 12 years have finally drawn to an end. I feel liberated and at peace.'

He also referred to the act of penitence through his sadbhavna fasts in 2011 after the Supreme Court initially exonerated him.

Modi and his supporters felt the need to clear the air about the 2002 anti-Muslim riots, show themselves to have been fair and refute the charge that Modi and BJP were anti-Muslim.

At the end of what appeared to be a one-man campaign for BJP, Modi wrote in his blog on 10 May 2014, titled 'Extensive, Innovative, Satisfying: The Story of 2014 Campaign':

Since September 13th 2013 when the responsibility of being the BJP's PM candidate was given to me, I have been travelling along the length and breadth of India. Friends in the party told me that I have addressed rallies and programmes in almost 5800 locations, covering a distance of over 3 lakh kilometres. The number of rallies I have addressed in this campaign season is 440 including the Bharat Vijay Rallies that I began with the blessings of Maa Vaishno Devi [on] 26th March 2014.

Modi managed to make the 2014 Lok Sabha election into a Modi election, and BJP was pushed into the background. Those who wanted to vote against Congress, against the Manmohan Singh government, were voting not for BJP but for Modi. Many in the media were quite overwhelmed by the domineering presence of

Modi and described the election as a presidential one as in the United States, and they pitted Congress Vice-President Rahul Gandhi against Modi. The media had unwittingly created the image of the seasoned politician Modi against a greenhorn Rahul.

In the 2004 election, it was not the personality of Prime Minister Atal Bihari Vajpayee that was in focus but the achievements of the BJP-led NDA government, and the Congress-led UPA did not even have a prime ministerial candidate, though it was Congress President Sonia Gandhi who had campaigned extensively and vigorously for the party. In 2009, BJP's prime ministerial candidate Advani and Congress's Manmohan Singh were not the leading gladiators, but it was the parties that were in the power duel. The media lionized Modi because it made for a simple picture, especially in the TV news channels, and the complexity of a national election was reduced to the image of the leader. This was not happening for the first time in India. Indira Gandhi turned the election of 1971 as one which was about her, but she had a substantial populist programme to offer the people. Modi only had a vague promise of generating employment for the youth and nothing more. Although the actual number of seats won by BJP—283—which was 11 more than the majority and a 31 per cent vote share reflected a modest mandate, Modi was success-ful in projecting it as his victory, though he thanked the foot soldiers profusely. There was a trace of Modi wave, though not an actual one.

Again, after the victory, friendly Modi-watchers predicted that his would be a presidential style of government, and that it would not be the cabinet form of government where the prime minister was first among the equals. It has indeed been the case that the prime minister has always been the key man and the rest of the cabinet ministers have been mere entourage. There have always been clashes between senior members of the cabinet and the prime minister, and the senior would resign in protest. Even Indira Gandhi, who seemed to have attained the status of 'the only leader', had to contend with the leaders who did not agree with her. Modi was all set to dominate and rule alone.

And he also took control of the party, and he had his confidante, Amit Shah, who engineered a spectacular win for the party by getting 73 out of the 80 Lok Sabha seats, made president of the BJP. He came to control both government and party, somewhat on the lines of Nehru, Indira and Rajiv. BJP had transformed itself into a copy of Congress. It found a strong leader who could lead the party to victory, and who would be the unchallenged leader of government and party.

BJP for a long time felt that unlike Congress, it had no charismatic leader with a nationwide appeal and that was one of the reasons it had not become a powerful national party, though it had its presence across the country, like the communist parties. The secret of power, it felt, was in finding a national leader. Modi fitted the bill. What limits Modi's power is not the party and its organizational structure, not his cabinet colleagues, but his own ability and his own imagination.

Modi's will to power has swept many off their feet. As BJP national spokesperson wrote in an article on 23 May 2014:

> Modi's campaign schedule ran on time, bucking the notorious trend of public meetings running behind schedule. Between rallies, Modi also gave media interviews. There were a few motivational sessions with party workers and strategy meetings with senior leaders. He also met diplomats, new allies and concerned citizens. The long working hours and the sheer diversity of activities that required his involvement needed high energy levels and Modi was up for the challenge. His energy helped us beat monotony, labour and the heat.

In May 2014, BJP and the NDA government stood in the shadow of Modi. •

MISSING CRESCENDO

With an impressive electoral victory behind him, which seemed bigger than it was because between 1989 and 2009 no party had managed to win even a simple majority in the Lok Sabha, though Prime Minister P.V. Narasimha Rao between 1991 and 1996 managed through successive stratagems to get around the problem, Modi for the first time in 25 years got to the comfortable perch of parliamentary majority. But between 2014 and 2019, it did not offer him any great advantage in governing the country. Parliamentary majority does not guarantee a successful government. What is irking Modi, his colleagues and his admirers in the party and outside is that he has not been able to do much more than remain in office without a scandal or crisis. There have been no dramatic achievements, something what Modi longed to do, not that he did not try to do the big and dramatic things.

His very first move as prime minister designate was to write to leaders of SAARC to attend his swearing-in ceremony on 26 May 2014 in New Delhi. It seemed an audacious, some called it imaginative, diplomatic opening move. No prime minister in any country who has won an election would call heads of state and government from the neighbourhood to attend a swearing-in ceremony which is usually seen as a domestic matter and, in a democracy, a routine change of guard. But the grand gesture did not lead to any dramatic change in India's relations with the SAARC neighbours, especially Bangladesh, Nepal, Pakistan and Sri Lanka.

In 2014 and 2015, he basked in the glory of his election victory. This was particularly evident when he addressed the Indian communities at the Madison Square Garden in New York on 28 September 2014, at the Allphones Arena in Sydney on

17 November 2014, at the SAP Center at San Jose on 27 September 2015 and his Townhall question and answer session with Mark Zuckerberg at the Facebook headquarters in Menlo Park in California.

He adopted a different tone, as he had to, when he addressed the Council on Foreign Relations in New York City on 29 September 2014, where there was the admixture of the elation of the electoral victory in May and India's need for foreign investment. Interpreting the electoral victory in his characteristically boastful tone, he said,

> The full majority government at Centre has suddenly renewed all the hopes and expectations of around two generations which were repressed till now.... Within first three months, we have been successful in improving our growth rate from 4.5 to 5.7 and its credit goes to an atmosphere of trust created after the formation of government, which in turn provides a tremendous boost to it.... As stated by Dr. Haass (Richard Haass, chairman of the Council on Foreign Relations), within a short span of three months we have secured a big Achievement in Mars mission. You would be pleased to know that our Space Scientists collected the small tools manufactured in small workshops of different states and gained success in reaching to Mars at a very low cost.

And from this, he argued the case of 'Make in India':

> The foreigners belonging to Manufacturing Sector need not analyse anything, but to conduct case study of our Mars mission and then realise if such a huge achievement can be made with the support of so skilled and cheap manpower, then why their products cannot be made in India. That's why we are emphasizing on 'Make in India' and Skill Development initiatives.

He pointed out that his government had then allowed 100 per cent foreign investment in Indian Railways, and that 'trillions

and trillions of business is linked only with Railways of India.'
And his final plea was: 'I've manpower and you have money. I've
talent and you have business experience. By combining both,
we can for sure accomplish this task to bring a phenomenal
change in the life of 125 crore Indians.' Modi spoke a language
that businessmen understand everywhere, with an element of
brashness and simplification in it. He was looking to accomplish
more than he could.

Speaking at the World Economic Forum at Davos on 23 January
2018, he once again made a sales pitch for foreign investments
in India. He said,

> Today, the way we are making Indian economy suitable
> for investment, there is no match to it. Consequently,
> today, investing in India, travelling to India, working in
> India, manufacturing in India, and exporting products
> and services from India to the world, everything has
> become much easier than before. We have tried to get rid
> of licence–permit raj. By removing the red tape we are
> laying red carpet. Almost all sectors of economy are open
> to Foreign Direct Investment. More than 90 per cent of the
> investment from automatic route is possible.

Between the aspirations of the prime minister and the government and the economic reality falls the shadow, which should
not be surprising because reality does not always tally with the
best laid plans. The shift in the tone of the annual Economic
Survey presents the economic mood of the nation as it were.
In 2014–2015, the survey exulted:

> As the new government presents its first full-year budget,
> a momentous opportunity awaits. India has reached a
> sweet spot—rare in the history of nations—in which it could
> be finally launched on a double-digit medium-term
> growth trajectory. This trajectory would allow the country
> to attain the fundamental objectives of 'wiping every tear
> from every eye' of the still poor and vulnerable, while
> affording the opportunities for the increasingly young,

middle class and aspirational India to realise its limitless potential.

In 2015–2016, there was a shift to a more cautious and realistic outlook:

> If the world economy lurches into crisis or slides into further weakness, India's growth will be seriously affected, for the correlation between global and Indian growth has been growing dramatically. Assessments of India's performance over the coming year will therefore need to be conditional. This is not an advance apology for likely future performance but the sobering reality of India becoming 'so entwined' with the world.

In 2016–2017, there was good news on the home front: 'Despite global headwinds and a truant monsoon, India registered robust growth of 7.2 per cent in 2014–15 and 7.6 per cent in 2015–16, thus becoming the fastest growing major economy in the world.'

The 2017–2018 report card of the economy that the survey recorded was one of temporary shock and pain. It said:

> Macroeconomic developments this year are marked by swings. In the first half, India's economy temporarily 'decoupled', decelerating as the world accelerated—even as it remained the second-best performer amongst major countries, with strong macroeconomic fundamentals. The reason lay in the series of actions and developments that buffeted the economy: demonetization and teething difficulties in the new GST, high and rising real interest rates, and intensifying overhang from the TBS (Twin Balance Sheet, which refers to the non-performing assets (NPAs) of the public sector banks) challenge, and sharp falls in certain food prices that impacted agricultural incomes.... In the second half of the year, the economy witnessed robust signs of revival. Economic growth improved as the shocks began to fade. Corrective actions were taken, and the synchronous global economic recovery boosted exports.

The most controversial and peremptory decision of Modi has been demonetization of ₹500 and ₹1,000 notes in a bid to fight 'corruption, black money and terrorism', which he had announced on 8 November 2016, when the economy seemed to be sailing smoothly but without any dramatic peaks. He said, 'There comes a time in the history of a country's development when a need is felt for a strong and decisive step.' And the 'big step' was: 'To break the grip of corruption and black money, we have decided that the five hundred rupee and thousand rupee currency notes presently in use will no longer be legal tender from midnight tonight, that is 8th November 2016.' Modi also offered a pseudo-economic argument about excess cash in the system: 'The magnitude of cash in circulation is directly linked to the level of corruption. Inflation becomes worse through the deployment of cash earned in corrupt ways.'

People were given 50 days' time to deposit ₹500 and ₹1,000 notes in exchange of smaller currency. This created a liquidity crisis of two kinds. First, people felt the cash crunch as they returned the high currency notes and the banks did not have enough of the small denomination notes to give in exchange. Second, the banks were flushed with excess liquidity, and the people did not have enough for their regular transactions.

In its annual report of 2016–2017, the Reserve Bank of India noted blandly:

> The value of bank notes in circulation declined by 20.2 per cent over the year to ₹13.102 billion as at end-March 2017. The volume of bank notes, however, increased by 11.1 per cent, mainly due to higher infusion of banknotes of lower denomination in circulation following the demonetization. In value terms, the share of ₹500 and above bank notes, which had together accounted for 86.4 per cent of the total value of banknotes in circulation at end-March 2016, stood at 73.4 per cent at end-March 2017. The share of newly introduced ₹2000 banknotes in the total value of banknotes in circulation was 50.2 per cent at end-March 2017. In volume terms, ₹10 and ₹100 banknotes

constituted 62.0 per cent of banknotes in circulation at end-March 2017 as compared with 53.0 per cent at end-March 2016.

The Economic Survey for 2016–2017 had a difficult task explaining demonetization because it could not be too critical of the measure nor question its economic rationale.

In Chapter 'Demonetisation: To Deify or Demonize', with quotations from Ramakrishna Paramahamsa, 'Taka mati, mati taka (Money is mud, mud is money)', to George Eliot in her novel *Middlemarch*, 'Among all forms of mistake, prophecy is the most gratuitous', the Economic Survey for 2016–2017 prefaced its analysis with the observation:

> Demonetisation has been a radical, unprecedented step with short term costs and long term benefits. The liquidity squeeze was less severe than suggested by the headlines and has been easing since end-December 2016. A number of follow-up actions would minimize the costs and maximise the benefits of demonetization. These include: fast, demand-driven remonetisation; further tax reforms, including bringing land and real estate into the GST; reducing tax rates and stamp duties; and allay anxieties about over-zealous tax administration. These actions should allow growth to return to trend in 2017–18, following a temporary decline in 2016–17.

And it followed this by the description:

> In the wake of the Global Financial Crisis (GFC), advanced economies have used monetary policy to stimulate growth, stretching its use to domains heretofore considered heretical such as negative interest policies and 'helicopter drops' of money. In fact, India has given a new expression to unconventional monetary policy, with the difference that whereas advanced economies have focused on expanding the money supply, India's demonetisation has reduced it. This policy could be considered

'reverse helicopter drop', or perhaps more accurately a 'helicopter hoover'.

The GDP growth rates tell a tale of a relatively stable economy without scaling spectacular peaks or falling too far low. In 2014–2015, the economy grew by 7.5 per cent compared to the last year of UPA government's growth rate of 6.4 per cent. In 2015–2016, the growth touched the peak of 8 per cent, and it fell to 7.1 per cent (according to Revised Estimates) in 2016–2017 and to 6.5 per cent (according to Advanced Estimates) in 2017–2018.

The state of the economy becomes the focal point of the Modi term because he himself set the task of development rather than Hindutva as the main plank of his government and of his party. There have been vigorous attempts to bring the people into the institutional framework through the Jan Dhan Yojana scheme, which involves opening bank accounts for the poor as part of financial inclusivity, supplying free gas cylinders to the poor through the Ujjwala scheme and near doubling of those who filed tax returns and of the direct tax collections, which present an impressive performance, but it falls below the expectations of Modi because he is not satisfied with anything less than spectacular. Modi is disappointed that he has not been able to do that one big thing that could be his claim to fame. Demonetization failed, though the government does not believe that it has, and the Goods and Services Tax (GST) is yet to stabilize.

EPILOGUE

Dream and Reality

The 35 years that span the prime ministerial terms of Rajiv Gandhi (1984–1989) and Narendra Modi (2014–2019) have not been smooth, even as the leaders and people struggled to move forward and bring about changes in the working of the economic and political system as old issues continued to drag back the forward movement.

Society, polity and the economy have witnessed enormous, and sometimes radical, changes during this period. And not all the changes have been inspiring. What really marks the India between Rajiv Gandhi and Narendra Modi has been the aspirational surge of the people, which pundits have interpreted in naively enthusiastic terms, but which has stayed the course despite the many obstacles on the way. To a great extent, governments have reflected the dreams and demands of the people, though the success rate has been modest.

I

The growth rate in the Rajiv Gandhi years had been 4.1 per cent in 1985–1986, 4.0 in 1986–1987, 4.0 in 1987–1988, 10.5 in 1988–1989 and 6.1 in 1989–1990. The economy had shown much resilience where industrial growth in a drought year buoyed up the growth momentum. Crisis was round the corner in 1991 as the first Gulf War against Iraq broke out in January 1991, and oil prices shot up, which became the main trigger for the 1991 economic crisis.

Economic reforms unspooled in 1991 have not been a magic formula. They have not banished economic problems, including crises in India and abroad. The euphoria about Indian economic reforms that policy-makers, economic analysts and free market ideologues felt was not reflected in the state of the economy over these years.

The immediate effect of economic reforms seems to have been positive but not too radical. The Economic Survey for 1997–1998 said:

> The average rate of growth of the economy rose from 6 per cent per annum in the Seventh Plan (1985–90) to 6.8 per cent in Eighth Plan (1992–97). Growth averaged a high of 7.5 per cent per annum in the last three years of the Eight Plan (1994–95 to 1996–97).

In 1997–1998, it fell to 5 per cent.

Presenting the Union Budget on 27 February 1999, NDA's Finance Minister Yashwant Sinha had to sum up the decade briefly and accurately: 'The decade of the nineties has witnessed extraordinary changes. It began with the collapse of the centrally planned economies. It is ending with market economies facing a serious crisis.'

And he gave a vivid description of the market crisis:

> The year 1998 particularly has been a year of unprecedented global turmoil. The East Asian financial crisis took a heavy toll of important economies in the region and spread to other countries. Japan continued in recession and in August 1998 severe crisis afflicted Russia. By January 1999, the contagion has spread to Brazil triggering massive capital flight and a steep depreciation of the currency. World output growth dropped below 2%, the growth of the world trade decelerated sharply, commodity prices fell steeply, currencies were savaged and capital flows to developing countries declined sharply.

Sinha said that India had to face economic sanctions because of the May 1998 Pokhran explosions. He claimed that in 1998–1999, the economy had grown at 5.8 per cent compared to 5 per cent of the previous year. He admitted that this growth was led by the 5.3 per cent growth in agriculture and allied sectors.

In the Budget he presented on 28 February 2002, Sinha was constrained to note: 'World economic growth is estimated to have slowed down to 2.4 per cent in 2001 after seven consecutive years of higher growth. International terror and the global economic slowdown have been the saddest feature of the past year.'

And on the economic situation at home, he said:

> Despite the hostile economic and security environment, the economy has performed relatively well this year. After irregular monsoons in the previous two years an agricultural recovery was enabled by a relatively well distributed monsoon this year. Economic growth this year is expected to be 5.4 per cent: higher growth being constrained by the industrial slowdown.

There are the positive signs: inflation at a record low of 1.1 per cent, foreign exchange reserves over US$50 billion, food stocks at 'almost 60 million tonnes' and lower petroleum prices.

The one year that turned out to be positive and even miraculous for the NDA government on the economic front was 2003–2004. The Economic Survey noted the positive anomaly and gave the reason as well:

> Real Gross Domestic Product (GDP) is estimated to have grown at 8.1 per cent in 2003–04, buoyed by a strong agricultural recovery of 9.1 per cent from the drought-affected previous year. A growth rate higher than 8 per cent has been achieved in the past in only three years: 1967–68 (8.1 per cent), 1975–76 (9.0 per cent), and 1988–89 (10.5 per cent). However the higher than expected growth in 2003–04, like in the other three years referred to above, was on the back of a year of poor growth (4.0 per cent) due to an unfavourable monsoon and fall in agricultural production.

The first three years of the UPA government witnessed robust growth rates and Chidambaram spelled it out in his Budget speech of 2008, though for the first time he also talked of downside risks.

> Honourable Members! The India growth story, so far, has been an absorbing and inspiring tale.... In the first three years of the UPA Government, the Gross Domestic Product (GDP) increased by 7.5 per cent, 9.4 per cent and 9.6 per cent, resulting in an unprecedented average growth rate of 8.8 per cent.

There were dark clouds on the horizon and the finance minister referred to them: 'At the beginning of the year, the outlook for the global economy was benign.... However, since August 2007, the financial markets in the developed countries have witnessed considerable turbulence that has not yet abated. The consequences for developing countries are also not yet clear.'

In 2009, the world economic crisis was looming large over the Indian economy. Finance Minister Pranab Mukherjee, presenting the Interim Budget on 16 February 2009, talked of the situation on the brink:

> The global financial crisis which began in 2007 took a turn for the worse in September 2008 with the collapse of several international financial institutions, including investment banks, mortgage lenders and insurance companies. There has been a severe choking of credit since then and a global crash in stock markets. The slowdown intensified with the US, Europe and Japan sliding into recession. Current indications of the global situation are not encouraging. Forecasts indicate that the World economy in 2009 may fare worse than in 2008.

> A crisis of such magnitude in developed countries is bound to have an impact around the world. Most emerging market economies have slowed down significantly. India too has been affected. For the first nine months of the current year, the growth rate of exports has come down

to 17.1 per cent. According to the latest figures available, the industrial production has fallen by 2 per cent year-on-year basis in December 2008. In these difficult times, when most economies are struggling to stay afloat, a healthy 7.1 per cent rate of GDP growth still makes India the second fastest growing economy in the world.

To counter the negative fallout of the global slowdown on the Indian economy, our Government took prompt action by providing substantial fiscal stimulus. The two packages announced on December 7, 2008 and January 2, 2009, provide tax relief to boost demand and aim at increasing expenditure on public projects to create employment and public assets. In this context, the Government renewed its efforts to increase infrastructure investments. In the period from August 2008 to January 2009 alone, the Government accorded approval for 37 infrastructure projects worth ₹70 thousand crore.

And in his 28 February 2013 Budget speech, P. Chidambaram spoke in a grave tone:

Global economic growth slowed from 3.9 per cent in 2011 to 3.2 per cent in 2012. India is part of the global economy: our exports and imports amount to 43 per cent of GDP and two-way external sector transactions have risen to 108 per cent of GDP. We are not unaffected by what happens in the rest of the world and our economy too has slowed after 2010–11. In the current year, the CSO has estimated growth at 5 per cent while the RBI has estimated growth at 5.5 per cent. Whatever may be the final estimate, it will be below India's potential growth rate of 8 per cent. Getting back to that growth rate is the challenge that faces the country.

2003–2004 to 2007–2008 had been dream years of growth, but the periodic crisis could not be kept away. The growth rates in a market economy when the going is good are indeed good. But like fair weather which does not last, so too the good days of the market economy. That is why Pranab Mukherjee in his 2009 Budget speech quoted economist Amartya Sen:

> We also have to take note of Prof. Amartya Sen's observation and I quote 'along with old slogan of "growth with equity", we also need a new commitment towards "down turn with security", given the fact that occasional downturns are common—possibly inescapable—in market economies' unquote. Employment generation schemes have to be expanded and social security nets have to be strengthened to protect the vulnerable sections of our society.

Finance Minister Arun Jaitley struck an upbeat note in his Budget speech of 1 February 2018:

> Indian economy has performed very well since our government took over in May, 2014. India achieved an average growth of 7.5 per cent in first three years of our Government. Indian economy is 2.5 trillion dollar economy—seventh largest in the world. India is expected to become fifth largest very soon. On Purchasing Power Parity (PPP) basis, we are already the third largest economy.

India has had a smooth ride in the Modi years, but the external and internal challenges remain. The Modi government does not feel the need to reckon with the volatile economic reality in the country and in the world in an election year. But the economic challenges remain, though they have not been spelt out.

II

BJP in the late 1980s had begun to ride the tiger of the proposed Ram temple at the site of Babri Masjid in Ayodhya. It has turned out to be an albatross. The party is in an unenviable position. It cannot build the temple legally without the consent of Muslims. It cannot throw its political weight into arm-twisting the Muslim leaders to give in to the temple demand. And it cannot abandon the temple issue as it remains a part of its core agenda. For the BJP leaders, it is a realpolitik dilemma. They understand that in a democracy you cannot be a blatant law-breaker or a cynical partisan. BJP wants to be a Hindu party but without being seen as being unfair to Muslims and other religious minorities. It may practise intolerance and discrimination, but it does not want to flaunt it. The party defers to democratic etiquette and norms. After the demolition, Vajpayee had to use all the rhetorical skills at his command to show that the demolition was an unintended consequence, though the party was very much in favour of building the temple at the site of the mosque but through fair and legal means. In 1996, 1998 and 1999, BJP did not showcase the demolition as an act of Hindu triumphalism. It fought the elections on other nationalist issues. Revivalism has remained the underlying theme of the party's ideology. Revivalism in the BJP lexicon meant asserting India's national pride, for example, through economic progress, the success of the expatriate Indians, especially in the United States, the Pokhran II explosion in May 1998, and, of course, by invoking the glories of ancient—read Hindu—civilization. The party relegated the mosque–temple dispute to the background if not on grounds of principle but of calculated scruple.

During the years of NDA, BJP took shelter behind the argument that it had put aside its own core agenda—common civil code, abolition of Article 370 of the Constitution which confers special status on Jammu and Kashmir and the building of Ram temple in Ayodhya—because it did not have a majority of its own, and that it had to defer to the common agenda of the alliance. The party leaders maintain that they have not given up on their basic agenda, but they would revive it only when they get a majority on their own. They are now convinced that they are not ever likely to get a majority of their own.

To prove the point that he is not a Hindutva leader who believes in the proposition that faith is above law, the man who was at the helm of the party's Ayodhya agitation, Home Minister L.K. Advani, took an unexceptionable and tough stand when he was home minister. He issued a statement on 27 February 2002, where he took note of the serious developments in Ayodhya: 'The Vishwa Hindu Parishad has embarked on a course of action in Ayodhya which is fraught with dangerous consequences. Thousands are sought to be assembled in Ayodhya to take part in a mass exercise which can only lead to flagrant defiance of court orders.'

Advani declared that he was proud of his association with the 'Ayodhya movement' and what VHP was planning to do would cause damage to the 'great movement'. And he issued the warning: 'If, however, they persist in their present approach, the Government of India would not hesitate to take action against those who defy court orders or create problems for law and order.' The irony that he was in the position of VHP on 6 December 1992, and that he was now dealing with the situation from the other side, cannot be ignored.

On 30 September 2010, a three-judge Lucknow Bench of the Allahabad High Court delivered the verdict on the disputed Babri Masjid–Ram Janmabhoomi site. The judgment was complex because it divided the site among the three claimants, the Nirmohi Akhara, the Hindu Maha Sabha representing the deity Ram Lalla and the Sunni Waqf Board.

The order of the court said:

> Accordingly, all the three sets of parties, i.e. Muslims, Hindus and Nirmohi Akhara are declared joint title holders of the property/premises in dispute ... to the extent of one third share each for using and managing the same for worshipping. A preliminary decree to this effect is passed.

> However, it is further declared that the portion below the central dome where at present the idol is kept in makeshift temple will be allotted to Hindus in final decree.

> It is further directed that Nirmohi Akhara will be allotted share including that part which is shown by the name Ram Chabutra and Sita Rasoi in the said map.

> It is further clarified that even though all the three parties are declared to have one third share each, however if while allotting exact portions some minor adjustment in

the share is to be made and the adversely affected party may be compensated by allotting some portion of the adjoining land which has been acquired by the Central Government.

All the three parties had gone in appeal to the Supreme Court, and the High Court's decree was stayed by the apex court in May 2011.

BJP, in its statement on 30 September 2010, said:

> The judgement of the 3-Judge bench of the Allahabad High Court at Lucknow has been pronounced today. In so far as the judgement upholds the right of the Hindus to construct a temple at the Garbh-Grih, it is a significant step forward towards the construction of a grand temple at the birth place of Lord Rama. The expert opinion of the Archaeological Survey of India and other expert agencies engaged by it had clearly opined that there were remains of a Hindu religious structure where the disputed structure stood. The Bharatiya Janata Party believes that this verdict opens a New Chapter for National Integration and a new era for inter-community relations. The BJP is gratified that the nation has received the verdict with maturity.

It was silent on the court order decreeing the division of the disputed site into three parts of one-third each.

It is necessary to remember the facts that the High Court had summed up in the section called 'Gist of the Findings'. The Muslims and the secularists rejected the judgment. The Hindu organizations turned a blind eye to the unpalatable facts like no temple was destroyed to build the mosque and that both Hindus and Muslims failed to establish their title deed but hung on to that part of the order which allotted the portion under the central dome of the destroyed mosque with the makeshift temple to the Hindus. It is necessary to know that the court held that the disputed site was in joint possession of both Hindus and

Muslims, which is an irritant to the fanatical elements in both the communities.

The grounds as enumerated by the court are as follows:

 1. The disputed structure was constructed as mosque by or under orders of Babar.

2. It is not proved by direct evidence that premises in dispute including constructed portion belonged to Babar or the person who constructed the mosque or under whose orders it was constructed.

3. No temple was demolished for constructing the mosque.

4. Mosque was constructed over the ruins of temples which were lying in utter ruins since a very long time before the construction of mosque and some material thereof was used in construction of the mosque.

5. That for a very long time till the construction of the mosque it was treated/believed by Hindus that somewhere in a very large area of which premises in dispute is a very small part birth place of Lord Ram was situated, however, the belief did not relate to any specified small area within that bigger area specifically the premises in dispute.

6. That after some time of construction of the mosque Hindus started identifying the premises in dispute as exact birth place of Lord Ram or a place wherein exact birth place was situated.

7. That much before 1855 Ram Chabutra and Sita Rasoi had come into existence and Hindus were worshipping in the same. It was very, very unique and absolutely unprecedented situation that inside the boundary wall and compound of the mosque Hindu religious places were there which were actually being

worshipped along with offerings of Namaz by Muslims in the mosque.

8. That in view of the above gist of the finding at serial no. 7 both the parties Muslims as well as Hindus are held to be in joint possession of the entire premises in dispute.

9. That even though for the sake of convenience both the parties i.e. Muslims and Hindus were using and occupying different portions of the premises in dispute still it did not amount to formal partition and both continued to be in joint possession of the entire premises in dispute.

10. That both the parties have failed to prove commencement of their title hence by virtue of Section 110 Evidence Act both are held to be joint title holders on the basis of joint possession.

11. That for some decades before 1949 Hindus started treating/believing the place beneath the Central dome of mosque (where at present make sift temple stands) to be exact birth place of Lord Ram.

12. That idol was placed for the first time beneath the Central dome of the mosque in the early hours of 23.12.1949.

13. That in view of the above both the parties are declared to be joint title holders in possession of the entire premises in dispute and a preliminary decree to that effect is passed with the condition that at the time of actual partition by meets and bounds at the stage of preparation of final decree the portion beneath the Central dome where at present makeshift temple stands will be allotted to the share of the Hindus.

There was no trouble anywhere in the country after the judgment had been pronounced, though there was apprehension in the political and governmental circles that once again the nation would be caught in Hindu–Muslim riots as had happened in December 1992 and January 1993 in Mumbai and other parts of the country. Both Muslims and Hindus across the country did not pay much attention to the controversy that once threatened to polarize the country. 2010 India was a different country from that of 1992 India.

But the Ayodhya issue has resurfaced, and it is set to haunt Narendra Modi as it did Rajiv Gandhi. Rajiv Gandhi wished it to go away. It did not. Modi too wants to skirt around the issue because he does not want to be a prime minister who led the country because he built a temple. He knows that if it were to happen, history would write him down. He does not want that, but he does not know how to break away from the Hindu zealots. Modi's critics are convinced that he is a crypto-Hindutva zealot himself, an image that Modi does not want for himself. He has this dream of being a Hindu 'spiritual' leader of a prosperous and powerful India. He faces the challenge of squaring the circle of Hindu fanaticism. He did not fight and win the 2014 Lok Sabha election on the temple plank.

SUGGESTED READINGS

Chapter II Economic Reforms: Precursor to Inheritor
http://eparlib.nic.in/bitstream/123456789/3817/1/lsd_08_1_22-01-1985.pdf#search=22 January 1985

Chapter III Rajiv's Camelot: Blink of a Dream
Zaidi, A.M., and S.G. Zaidi. *The Encyclopaedia of the Indian National Congress.* 9–15 July 1991, Nos 1–5, Vol. 1; 24 July 1991, Nos 11–13, Vol. II, Lok Sabha Debates; 1991–1993, Vol. 28.

http://www.sikhtimes.com/doc_072485a.html
https://assam.gov.in/documents/1631171/0/Annexure_10.pdf?version=1.0
https://peacemaker.un.org/sites/peacemaker.un.org/files/IN_860630_Mizoram%20Accord.pdf
http://eparlib.nic.in/bitstream/123456789/319/1/lsd_08_1_30-01-1985.pdf#search=Anti-Defection Bill, 30 Jan 1985
https://archive.org/stream/selectedspeeches01gand/selectedspeeches01gand_djvu.txt

Chapter IV Rajiv's Fall: Furies Unleashed
http://eparlib.nic.in/bitstream/123456789/3803/1/lsd_08_5_25-02-1986.pdf#search=Muslim Women (Protection of Rights on Divorce) Bill, 1986
http://eparlib.nic.in/bitstream/123456789/385/1/lsd_08_14_12-10-1989.pdf#search=12 October 1989
http://eparlib.nic.in/bitstream/123456789/878/1/lsd_08_14_11-10-1989.pdf#search=11 October 1989, Home Minister Buta Singh
http://eparlib.nic.in/bitstream/123456789/3822/1/lsd_08_08_20-04-1987.pdf#search=Statement on Bofors 20 April 1987
http://eparlib.nic.in/bitstream/123456789/1446/1/lsd_08_11_29-08-1988.pdf#search=Anti-Defamation Bill, 29 August 1988
eparlib.nic.in/bitstream/123456789/914/1/lsd_08_14_25-07-1989.pdf#search=Bofors 25 July 1989

http://eparlib.nic.in/bitstream/123456789/459/1/lsd_08_13_15-05-1989.pdf#search=Panchayati Raj 15 May 1989
http://eparlib.nic.in/bitstream/123456789/869/1/lsd_08_14_13-10-1989.pdf#search=Valedictory Reference 13 October 1989

Chapter V The Traumatic Turn
Zaidi, A.M., and S.G. Zaidi. *The Encyclopaedia of the Indian National Congress*. Vol. 28, 1991–1993, S. Chand, New Delhi.

Chapter VI Ending the Free Fall
Zaidi, A.M., and S.G. Zaidi. *The Encyclopaedia of the Indian National Congress*. 1986–1990, Vol. 27; 1991–1993, Vol. 28.

Chapter VII Winds of Change
22–28 May, 1996, No. 1–5; 22 May–12 June, 1996, No. 1–8, Volume I, Lok Sabha Debates

Chapter VIII Ayodhya Agony
Lok Sabha Debates. 2–4 December 1992, Nos 7–9, Vol. XVI.

Chapter IX Apologetics of Vandalism
Lok Sabha Debates. 17–18 December 1992, Nos 14–15, Vol. XVII.

Chapter X BJP's Moment of Truth
Lok Sabha Debates. 22–28 May 1996, Nos 1–5; 22 May–12 June 1996, Nos 1–8, Vol. I.

Chapter XI Romancing Pakistan
Lok Sabha Debates. 20–29 October 1999, Nos 1–8, Vol. I.

Chapter XII The Bomb Gambit
Lok Sabha Debates. 27 May–2 June 1998, Nos 1–5, Vol. II.

Chapter XIII Love and War
Report No. 19 for the period ended March 2010 Performance Audit of Issue of Licences and Allocation of 2G Spectrum by the Department of Telecommunications (Ministry of Communications and Information Technology (http://saiindia.gov.in/english/home/Our_Products/Audit_Report/Government_Wise/union_audit/recent_reports/union_performance/2010_2011/Civil_%20Performance_Audits/Report_no_19/Report_no_19.html)

http://www.pib.nic.in/newsite/pmreleases.aspx?mincode=3
http://www.pib.nic.in/newsite/pmreleases.aspx?mincode=3
Report No. 7 of 2012-13 for the period ended March 2012 - Performance Audit of Allocation of Coal Blocks and Augmentation of Coal Production (Ministry of Coal)
http://saiindia.gov.in/english/home/Our_Products/Audit_Report/Government_Wise/union_audit/recent_reports/union_performance/2012_2013/Commercial/Report_No_7/Report_No_7.html

Chapter XIV General Bluffs, Agra Blues
Lok Sabha Debates. 23–25 July 2001, Nos 1–3, Vol. XVII.

Chapter XV Modi's Inferno
Lok Sabha Debates. 11–14 March 2002, Nos 11–14, Vol. 22;
www.aicc.org.in/new/sonia-speeches.php
www.aicc.org.in/new/sonia-speeches.php

Chapter XVI Sonia's Revenge
Union Budget Speech 2003, 2004
Press Information Bureau press releases 2004, 2006

Chapter XVII Manmohan's Finest Hour
Press Information Bureau press releases January 2004, July 2005
Lok Sabha Debates. 27 February–1 March 2006, Nos 8–10, Vol. 17.
Lok Sabha Debates. 21–22 July 2008, Nos 1–10, Vol. XXXV.

Chapter XVIII Spectre of Corruption
Department of Telecommunications, Ministry of Communications and Information Technology. *Performance Audit of Issue of Licences and Allocation of 2G Spectrum*. Report no. 19 for the period ended March 2010. Available at: http://saiindia.gov.in/english/home/Our_Products/Audit_Report/Government_Wise/union_audit/recent_reports/union_performance/2010_2011/Civil_%20Performance_Audits/Report_no_19/Report_no_19.html
http://www.pib.nic.in/newsite/pmreleases.aspx?mincode=3
Ministry of Coal. *Performance Audit of Allocation of Coal Blocks and Augmentation of Coal Production*. Report no. 7 of 2012–2013 for the period ended March 2012. Available at: http://saiindia.gov.in/english/home/Our_Products/Audit_Report/Government_Wise/

union_audit/recent_reports/union_performance/2012_2013/
Commercial/Report_No_7/Report_No_7.html
Dramatis Personae
Manmohan Singh, the Unquiet Liberal
http://www.pib.nic.in/newsite/pmreleases.aspx?mincode=3

XIX The Short Long March
http://www.bjp.org/en/media-resources/press-releases/
resolution-passed-by-bjp-parliament-board
http://www.bjp.org/en/media-resources/press-releases/press-
shri-m-venkaiah-naidu-on-pm-comment-on-shri-narendra-modi
http://www.bjp.org/en/media-resources/press-releases/article-
shri-arun-jaitley-on-qon-the-road-to-2014q
http://www.bjp.org/en/media-resources/press-releases/article-
shri-arun-jaitley-on-qwhy-is-the-congress-party-trying-to-
communalise-the-2014-electionsq
http://www.bjp.org/en/media-resources/press-releases/article-
shri-arun-jaitley-on-the-conspiracy-of-falsehood-stands-exposed
http://www.bjp.org/en/media-resources/press-releases/blog-
sh-narendra-modi-on-satyameva-jayate-truth-alone-triumphs
http://www.bjp.org/en/media-resources/press-releases/blog-
shri-narendra-modi-on-extensive-innovative-and-satisfying-the-
story-of-2014-campaign-a
http://www.bjp.org/en/media-resources/press-releases/article-
smt-nirmala-sitharaman-on-modi-leads-from-the-front

Chapter XX Missing Crescendo
https://www.narendramodi.in/pms-address-and-interaction-
at-council-on-foreign-relations-in-new-york-city-6683
https://www.ndtv.com/india-news/pm-narendra-modis-speech-
at-world-economic-forum-in-davos-full-text-1803790
https://www.indiabudget.gov.in/budget2015-2016/vol1_survey.asp
https://www.indiabudget.gov.in/budget2016-2017/vol1_survey.asp
https://www.indiabudget.gov.in/es2016-17/echapter.pdf
http://mofapp.nic.in:8080/economicsurvey/pdf/001-031_
Chapter_01_ENGLISH_Vol_01_2017-18.pdf
https://www.rbi.org.in/scripts/AnnualReportPublications.aspx?
Id=1235

Epilogue: Dream and Reality
http://www.indiabudget.nic.in/es97-98/
http://indiabudget.nic.in/es2003-04/esmain.htm
Lok Sabha Debates. 29 February 2000, No. 5, Vol. 4.
Lok Sabha Debates. 28 February 2001, No. 7, Vol. 14.
Lok Sabha Debates. 28 February 2002, No. 3, Vol. 22.
http://indiabudget.nic.in/ub2008-09/bs/speecha.htm
http://indiabudget.nic.in/ub2009-10%28I%29/bs/speecha.htm
http://elegalix.allahabadhighcourt.in/elegalix/ayodhyafiles/
honsukj.pdf
https://www.indiabudget.gov.in/ub2018-19/bs/bs.pdf

ABOUT THE AUTHOR

Hyderabad-born (1953), New Delhi-based journalist **Parsa Venkateshwar Rao Jr** has worked with *The Indian Express, India Today, The Gulf Today* (Sharjah), *The Straits Times* (Singapore), tehelka.com and *DNA* (Daily News and Analysis). He has written for *Gulf News* (Dubai), *The Daily Star* (Beirut), *Today* (Singapore), *Deccan Herald* (Bengaluru), the *New Indian Express, The Asian Age, Deccan Chronicle* and *The Times of India*. His earlier books include *Mullah Omar and Robespierre: Essays in the Politics of Ideas* (2005), *Lokpal: Facts & Arguments* (2011), *Indian Politics Since 1991: Reforms and Revivalism* (2013) and the *Emergency: An Unpopular History* (2017). At present, he is the Political Editor of *Parliamentarian*, a monthly political magazine, and a freelance journalist.

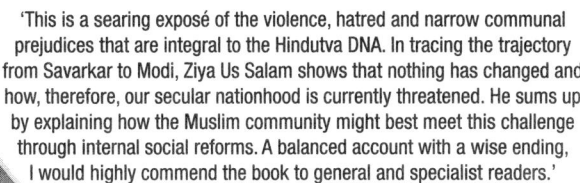

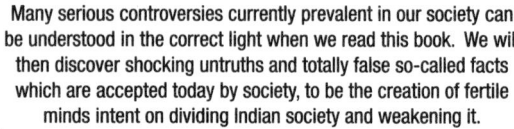